MARIE—
BEST WISHES
(signature)
10/06

How to Get Rich in Real Estate ... AND Have a Life!

What brokers want you to know that _most_ schools don't teach.

By

Wayne and Lynn Morgan
The Business School for Real Estate Pros

CICALA, Inc.

The Business School for Real Estate Pros™
Business Building and Investing Courses & Tools

1.

The Business Blueprint

A real estate Business

in a Box

2.

Customized lead-

generating Web Sites

3.

Fundamentals of

Business Building

3-Day Seminar

How to turn your

business into a lead-

generating machine

4.

Advanced Business-

Building Strategies

3-Day Seminar

How to put your business

on autopilot

5.

The Psychology

of Investing

3-Day Seminar

How to invest business

profits into low-risk,

high-yield properties

6.

The Masters Program

5-Day Advanced

Seminar

Taking it all to the

next level

More tools, reports and schedules available @ www.buildmybusiness.com

Dedication

This book is dedicated to real estate brokers and agents everywhere who have the courage to venture out into the unknown in search of a better life. The world is changing at a high rate of speed. What once seemed safe is now very risky, and what once seemed risky is now safe. There is no longer any such thing as a safe, secure job. Safety and security come from having the basic, fundamental business skills that allow one to thrive in business no matter what the economy or the competition is doing.

No one can make it on his or her own, so we also dedicate this work to the agents' families for their love, support, encouragement, and belief in them.

The desire to serve burns deep in the hearts of each and every agent.

May you be, do, and have all you desire.

From the two of us, who have been where you are, we also dedicate the following phrase:

"Real estate is the best business in the world. We help other people make their dreams come true ... while achieving our own."

—*Unknown*

Good luck to you in your business.

Acknowledgments

How do you thank everyone who deserves thanks?

First of all, I'd like to thank my wife, Lynn, who saved my life and makes me believe anything is possible; her parents, Henry and Mary Ellen Vandiver, for bringing her into this world; her sister, Pam, the best real estate salesperson in the world, and her husband, Barry; our nephews, Brett and Jeff, and Jeff's wife, Erica; our children, Lindsay, Shelly and her husband Aaron, and Brad; my parents, Don and Elaine Morgan; my brother Mike, the best big brother ever, and his wife, Belinda; and my sisters Rhonda, Holly, and Terri.

To all the top-notch staff and instructors of The Austin Institute of Real Estate and the graduates who have blessed us with their patronage. To JB Goodwin, mentor and friend; Hugh Parrish and Holland and Joyce Wiler for their undying support and technical advice; Missy DiDonato and Janis Cartwright for their initial guidance, help, and inspiration; my fellow instructors and dearest friends, Blair Singer, Brendan Nichols, Tony Fogarty, and Dominic Lione; and to Keith Cunningham for his friendship, advice, and counsel. Also to Jayne Johnson for assisting with clarity, and dear friends Pauline Abel and Krystyna Spicer.

Special thanks to Robert and Kim Kiyosaki for their inspiration and encouragement, and leading the way.

Authors' Note

This book is an exposé about the real estate business.

It was written by insiders: two brokers who have many years of success and experience in the varied aspects of real estate. They have had experience as listing brokers representing sellers; as buyers' brokers representing buyers; as managers, having managed the largest branch office for the largest real estate brokerage company in the city; as investors, who have bought and sold many properties and have a sizable real estate portfolio; and as educators, whose real estate education company has trained tens of thousands of agents. The real estate education company, The Austin Institute of Real Estate, has a 70 percent market share and a proprietary training program no other real estate school offers. The Austin Institute of Real Estate is located in Austin, Texas, and is known locally as "The Business School for Real Estate Pros."

We are the brokers who have witnessed the pain, frustration, and aggravation of people who have failed in the business. It pains us to see intelligent, articulate, kind, generous people spend so much time, effort, and money to obtain their license only to leave the business a short time later.

We never knew why the attrition was so high until we bought a real estate school. After we acquired it, we saw the business from the education side. We saw what we had never seen before.

From this new perspective, we saw that the real estate licensing exams have very little to do with real world real estate. The exams were created, for the most part, by people who have never been successful in real estate and have little, if any, knowledge of what agents really need to know to be successful.

The real estate schools fulfill their function well, which is to prepare students for the licensing exam.

Obtaining the real estate license guarantees nothing. It is merely the entry fee an agent pays to get into the game. It gets the agent on to the field, but it does not give him or her the skills he or she needs to compete.

That's why most people fail. They think, with good reason, that if they get their license, that is all they need.

This book was written because the real estate business is the best business in the world; it is fulfilling, rewarding, and very, very lucrative.

It is also, with the right education, very simple.

It is also relatively easy. It requires no special degree or years of formal education. Anyone who is committed enough and follows the three steps can do it.

Obtaining the license is just the first step of the Three-Step Success System we have developed.

Step One is obtaining the license.

Step Two is building the business.

Step Three is investing the profits into real estate.

We hated seeing people fail, especially when we know how to be successful in this business. That's why we wrote this book and created all the seminars that accompany it.

Whether you are considering getting into real estate, have just entered the business, or have been in it awhile and want to make more money and work fewer hours, this book and the Business Blueprint will show you how to design and build a business that works ... so you don't have to.

This book is about making money and converting that income into a passive income stream that flows in to you whether you work or not.

It is also about life after getting money handled.

Have you ever thought that there might be more to your life than just making money?

Our belief is that everyone arrived on earth with a special gift—something valuable to give to their fellow human beings. However, many people never realize their gift, as they get caught up in "earning a living" rather than doing what they are supposed to be doing.

We provide these tools in hopes that you will get out of the struggle of earning a living and go out and fulfill your life's purpose. The world needs you and your gift.

Table of Contents

Introduction

The educational system as a whole in this country has failed miserably. If I were grading it, I would have to give it an F.

The real estate schools do no more to prepare real estate agents for real estate than formal education does to prepare people for life.

The licensing process is simple. All one has to do is pass the state licensing exam. Unfortunately, the exam was created by employees who have never listed or sold any real estate and therefore have no knowledge of what agents really need to know. I have never had a buyer ask me how many square feet are in an acre or how many cubic yards of concrete are in a driveway, and those questions (and the answers) never made me any money. They are, however, on the state licensing exam.

There Are Two Parts to Learning

Agents are forced to memorize irrelevant answers to these questions and many other obscure facts in order to demonstrate their "competency" to governmental licensing entities. In the eyes of most real estate commissions, one is deemed "competent" when he or she has passed the state exam.

Unfortunately, they enter the business unprepared. They have mastered the technical side of the business, but have no skills in the practical side. Sitting indoors memorizing answers will get someone through the state licensing exam, but it will not prepare anyone for the business.

If the Student Didn't Learn ...

It's not that the licensing information is totally irrelevant. Before you get started in this business, it's important to know what forms to use and how to fill them out. Therefore, having a Law and Contracts course is a good idea.

A new agent also needs to understand the principles of real estate as well as those of agency.

What agents also need to know is that this is technical information and that it is being taught by school owners who, for the most part, have never listed or sold any real estate either. They have little to no experience in the subjects they are teaching.

I made less than $5,000 during my first year in the business. I was very disappointed to learn that my good grades in class and high marks on the state exam did not translate into financial success in the real world.

After obtaining my license and failing to attract either buyers or sellers who would use my services, I went back to the school where I received my initial education. I asked them how to go about getting buyers to call me and allow me to represent them or how to get sellers to allow me to market their homes.

I was stunned at their response to my request for help. "We don't know that part of the business. We have never listed or sold any real estate. We just teach the required classes." It is surprising how many inexperienced "teachers" are "teaching."

> There are two fundamental problems in education:
> 1. What is taught
> 2. The way it is taught

The first problem is that we have licensing exams being created by people with no real success in the business, and the information on those exams is sometimes taught by people who have little or no success in the business. No wonder the failure rate is so high. The system of education is flawed. Most people enter the real estate business without the basic fundamental skills necessary to be successful. Unfortunately, they don't know that. They think they are ready because they made good grades on the test. They were told what to learn, and they learned it. However, they need to know more.

The second problem is that people are just not educated. It is not that people can't learn. The problem is that they are often taught irrelevant, obsolete information by instructors who don't have the skills to teach and have no experience in that field.

Lecturing is NOT teaching.

Sitting still and listening to someone talk and memorizing what he or she says isn't learning; instead, it is recording. Students have become recording devices, and there is little understanding of the subject matter. They just record what is being said and replay it on cue. This is not education.

As schools across the country continue to lower their standards, more and more illiterates are being graduated without even the basic fundamentals of how to read and write. Take for example a local high school principal who, when asked why his students could not pass the state competency exam required for graduation, was quoted as saying, "Our biggest problem is, can the kids read it [the test] in order to put down the right answer? I would wager that they can't."

The following excerpt from *Business Week* highlights the pitfalls in this country's education system.

From his first days in school, an average boy is already developmentally two years behind the girls in reading and writing. Yet he's often expected to learn the same things in the same way in the same amount of time. While every nerve in his body tells him to run, he has to sit still and listen for almost eight hours a day. Biologically, he needs about four recesses a day, but he's lucky if he gets one, since some lawsuit-leery schools have banned them altogether. Hug a girl and he could be labeled a "toucher" and swiftly suspended—a result of what some say is an anti-boy culture that pathologizes their behavior. If he falls behind, he's likely to be shipped off to special ed, where he'll find that more than 70% of his classmates are boys. Squirm, clown, or interrupt, and he is four times as likely to be diagnosed with attention deficit hyperactivity disorder. That often leads to being forced to take Ritalin or risk being expelled, sent to special ed, or having parents accused of negligence. One study of public schools in Fairfax County, Va., found that more than 20% of upper-middle-class white boys were taking Ritalin-like drugs by fifth grade.

Once a boy makes it to freshman year of high school, he's at greater risk of falling behind in grades, extracurricular activities, and advanced placement ... All the while, he's 30% more likely to drop out, 85% more likely to commit murder, and four to six times more likely to kill himself, with boy suicides tripling since 1970 (Business Week, May 26, 2003; ISSN 0007-7135).

Financial education is virtually nonexistent. Ninety-five percent of the people in this country who reach the age of sixty-five cannot put their hands on $10,000 cash after working for decades! Even the brightest students who specialize, have a high degree of technical ability, and go on to earn large incomes (doctors, lawyers, engineers) lack business skills, work too hard, work paycheck to paycheck, and worry about money.

The Educational System's Three Groups

The biggest problem is harder to spot and doesn't show up until later in life and often after it is too late to do anything about it. There are three groups of people who come out of the education system.

The first group is comprised of the uneducated. They don't know, and they know they don't know. They will take menial jobs, exchanging their labor for hourly wages in hopes of having a roof over their heads, a vehicle that will get them from point A to point B (or just ride the vehicle the city provides), and food and clothing.

The second group is the well educated. They know, and they know they know. They usually do well financially. Good education is a major focus, and housing, transportation, clothing, and food are handled. They live in a world of abundance. They usually live rather well, knowing how to advance in the world.

The last group is the mis-educated. These are the ones in trouble. They are in trouble because they think they know. The problem is what they know is not necessarily true. They memorized all the right answers. They made good grades. The problem is the answers they memorized were wrong. They hit middle age, and the picture they had when they were young and the reality they have now are two very different pictures. Times have changed. Their specialty is no longer needed. They are being replaced by technology and/or younger, fresher (cheaper) minds.

The school system is a factory, and the product is employees. The end product is people who will be good (sit still, behave, and be easy to manage), do as they are told (do not think for yourself), make good grades (memorize old, obsolete, irrelevant information), get a good job, and work hard (become a slave) for money (but never acquire any wealth). This is a recipe for financial disaster.

Students are learning less and less, as they "graduate" from school having memorized enough "right answers" in a system that continuously lowers its standards. This practice is costing billions of dollars each year in lost productivity and increased training expenses as companies take on the teachers' job of training their employees in the basics of reading and writing, communication, math, manners, and socialization.

The Long-Term Effect

Most agents see real estate as an easy way to make a lot of money. They are right. It is, but you have to have the skills to play the game. You must commit to becoming a lifelong learner.

Most agents entering the business do not have the basic skills because their educational system did not teach them. The school they went to taught them what was on the test so they could get the license, not build a business—add to that the fact that most students by now have developed a severe dislike for the education process. Therefore, they only take the minimum amount of courses required to get started and end up not being as prepared as well as they could be to be a real player in the game.

They were not taught marketing, sales, negotiations, or how to keep a set of books, account for their income and expenses, read financial statements, or invest. They were mis-educated. They think they know. Like I mentioned before, the license is merely the entry fee one pays to enter the game. It gets you onto the playing field. It does not teach you the skills required to win.

It is no wonder the failure rate in real estate is close to 90 percent.

The truth is that the real estate industry is an easy business in which to get rich. All you have to do is find someone who wants to own a house, find one he or she likes, and show him or her how to pay for it. Or, find someone who wants to sell his or her home and show him or her how to sell it. Do that well and ask for referrals. Invest the profits into low-risk, high-yield investment properties. The simpler you keep it, the richer you will get.

This book is about how we got rich in real estate ... and how you can, too.

TESTIMONIALS

"As a presenter, you are, in our opinion, one of the best in the world … Thank you for the energy, effort, and enormous skill that you put into keeping audiences of 150 on the edge of their seats for 3½ days."

Diane McCann – Owner

Accelerated Business Technologies PTY LTD

Adelaide, Australia

"Wayne Morgan has the powerful ability to inspire people to go beyond their personal limits, and quite often have a good time doing it."

Dominique Lyone – Owner

Complete Office Supplies

Sydney, Australia

"… Thank you for being a committed and dynamic presenter who successfully provoked my thinking and extended my intellectual creativity."

Isabelle Adams – Ministry of Education

Perth (South) District

Perth, Australia

* *

"I learned more from you in 3½ days than I learned in 4 years at Harvard University, and I have a master's and Ph.D. in education."
Dr. Mary Ann bin Sallik – Professor of Aboriginal Studies
University of Adelaide
Adelaide, Australia

"Close to 1,000 students have now experienced the excellence of your teaching here in Melbourne alone. The impact you are having on the businesses of Victoria is sure to have a major influence on resurrecting our battered economy."
Jane Jordan – Partner
Wilson Jordan Group
Melbourne, Australia

"Wayne is more than a trainer; he is a long-term educator who leaves his attendees with retention value rather than motivational hype—and what a difference that makes to the bottom line."
Sue Saliba – Owner
Computel
Perth, Australia

Part One

Why the Licensing Process Does Not Work

Chapter One

The Typical Agent

Jana awoke at the sound of the alarm clock with a silent groan. Another day was about to begin. It was another day of rushing through her morning routine and getting ready for work. It was another day of sitting in traffic, watching others do the same, and wondering why anyone in his or her right mind would do this. Another day of trying to please the boss she was now convinced she couldn't please. It wasn't that she hated her job. Actually, she didn't mind it so much. The office was neat and clean. The people she worked with were, for the most part, happy and upbeat. The pay was decent. After all, it wasn't like she was some kind of highly qualified specialist the company needed for continued growth. She knew she should feel fortunate to have a good job, to live in a place that was prospering, with low unemployment, where jobs were plentiful, people were kind to each other, and living conditions were good. The truth be known, she often felt pangs of guilt when feelings of being unfulfilled overcame her.

"You should be happy," she would say to herself. "Look at all you have: an adoring husband; two beautiful, smart, healthy kids; lots of friends; and a wonderful home and lifestyle."

She felt bad for feeling bad. Somehow, though, it just wasn't working out. She found herself humming a song from her past and asking herself, "Is that all there is?" The light changed. Lost in thought, she envisioned a different life—a life of joy, a life of fun, a life of looking forward to tomorrow, a life with some meaning to it, more meaning than just earning a paycheck. Her mind began to wander, and with nothing else to do, she let it go.

"What if I could have my life exactly the way I wanted it?" she thought to herself. Immediately, her mind responded, "No way," and gave her all of the reasons why she couldn't have it. Even so, she persisted.

"What if ..." The horn honking behind and the sight of the SUV's grill in her rearview mirror brought her back to her senses. She accelerated through the light and continued her journey to work. "TGIF," she thought to herself as she looked forward to the weekend. "Tomorrow, I get to relax." The thought of a better life faded as she glanced at her watch. "I better hurry, or I'm going to be late." Besides, what else was she going to do?

She was about to find out. That afternoon, she was downsized.

One Door Closes ...

As Jana drove home that day after work, she was on an emotional roller coaster. She ran the gamut of emotions from the hurt of rejection to the insult of being inadequate to the embarrassment of being let go and having to explain that to the relief of not having to go back there ever again. She was also somewhat excited, though uncertain, of what the future may hold.

"I'll check Sunday's paper, take a few weeks off, casually look around, and see what comes up," she thought to herself.

Her husband, Bill, was supportive as always. "Fools," he told her. "They're fools to let you go. Anyone would be happy to have you in their organization. I know I would." He continued to blast the company through dinner, but Jana only heard part of it. Her mind was elsewhere, planning the future.

Saturday was a blur, spent hauling the kids from activity to activity. Soccer, band practice, and a friend's birthday party made the day go by quickly. Suddenly, Sunday was upon them, and Jana arose early as usual for her favorite ritual of the week: coffee and the Sunday paper. The whole family knew that this was one of her few luxuries, and they were always considerate and gave her time and space.

Jana loved to read the Sunday paper from cover to cover, devouring it, soaking it up like sunshine on a warm spring day. She sipped her coffee as she read one section after the other, slowly, methodically working her way through the oversized Sunday edition. Eventually, there she was, with the classifieds.

"I wonder what I want to be when I grow up?" she thought to herself with an impish grin. "Let's see what the world has to offer." As she read through the columns, she imagined herself in each position, allowing for the possibility for some, discounting others outright. Accounting, administration, bookkeeping, clerical—she read them all, looking for something that sounded new and promising. Nothing caught her eye or her imagination. Management, professional, sales …

Most of it sounded like old, tired hype, all the same. She was folding the paper up when she spotted it.

"Be your own boss." It read, "Control your own time; unlimited income potential. Real estate agents needed for new office expansion. Training included, leads provided."

She recalled the real estate agent who sold them their home. The agent was very professional, well dressed, well informed, and was articulate and handled herself and their transaction quite well.

Jana remembered being impressed with her and wondered what happened to her, if she was even still in the business.

Free at Last ...

The ad intrigued her. She could be her own boss. That was one thing she had never considered. She just always assumed she would have a boss, someone she had to answer to, put up with, and explain things to. It was all part of having a job. If you have a job, you have a boss. The two went hand in hand. To not have a boss? She considered what that might be like. To have no one to tell her what to do, or ask her what she had done, or why, or why not, or anything else. She had to admit, that part sounded good. Also, the part about "control your own time." That was something she never seemed to have enough of. She was constantly saying to herself and others, "I just don't have enough time." The possibility of being able to control of her time took some getting used to. She could get up whenever she wanted, go to lunch at her leisure, and stop work when she got tired.

She could even take a nap in the middle of the day! A weekday! Have lunch with her friends. What a concept! She was beginning to like this idea more and more. "It's a sign!" she thought. She decided to call first thing Monday morning.

Seize the Moment ...

"What about that 'take a few weeks off and rest?'" asked Bill, although he already knew the answer to the question.

He had seen this before and had been married to Jana long enough to recognize the pattern. She had just kicked into "high intensity" mode and was traveling at warp speed. Ready, fire ... aim! It always annoyed him that she did not take time to analyze things before she did them. She often created as many problems as she solved, but, he had to admit, she got more done in less time than any three people he knew.

"I have no job, remember?" she shot back. "Besides, I want to hear what these people have to say." Then she softened. "Honey, I have been thinking about getting into real estate for years. We've talked about that. I love looking at houses, and after all, how hard could it be? The kids will be in college before we know it, and college is not going to be cheap. And we keep talking about going to Europe. Are our dreams only going to be dreams, or are we going to make them come true? We paid that woman—I don't even remember her name—over $12,000 to sell our house, and what did she do? She put up a sign, hung that lock thing on our front door, and scratched it up, remember that? And we didn't see her again until closing.

Honey, I only need to sell one a month, and I could triple my income! Paris, here we come! Yale, get ready; my kids are on the way!"

The last thing Bill wanted to do was dampen her spirit. That was one of the things that attracted him to Jana in the first place. She had that ever-present, positive, cheerful, "can do" attitude that he loved. Torn between being realistic and being supportive, he said the only thing a true partner could say.

"Well, if that's what you want to do, go check it out. What's the next step?"

"I'm calling the number in the ad," she said, "and I'll let you know." Two nights later, they were at an evening seminar learning what it takes to get started in real estate.

Another Door Opens ...

Jana was so excited that she didn't want to leave the meeting. Her head was spinning with dozens of questions as she considered all the possibilities for her future. She never knew that getting her real estate license could be so easy. The broker was going to train her and provide leads and marketing materials and ads as well. "I should have done this a long time ago," she thought to herself as she added up all the commissions she was going to make from all the people she knew. Talk about a sphere of influence! She could hardly sit in her seat! She thought about all her skills, all the different jobs she had over the years, and all her experiences.

As she listened to the presentation, she had this feeling that she was finally in the right place at the right time. All those past experiences had been a preparation for this.

As she and Bill drove home, she felt different. She was experiencing feelings she had never felt before, and she was excited about all the possibilities. On the other hand, there was also some anxiety, nervousness, and even some fear as she thought about venturing out into the unknown. She had to take a few classes, prepare for the state licensing exam, and take the test, all of which she could accomplish in just twenty-one days! With a head full of new information, a new language on her tongue, and a song in her heart, Jana had just become the city's newest potential real estate licensee!

And a Journey Begins ...

Her heart leapt with joy as she left the exam center clutching her exam test results. She was on her way! She had completed her courses, studied diligently, and learned the language of real estate. All the new terms and definitions that seemed so convoluted and confusing at first were now clear as a bell. She knew the difference between accretion and erosion! Easement and encroachment! Warranty deed versus general deed! Joint tenants and tenants in common!

She could figure metes and bounds and could tell you to the gram how many cubic yards of concrete were in the driveway and sidewalk. She scored in the top percentile! Jana was proud of herself and her accomplishments. She couldn't wait to get home and tell Bill!

That night, they had a celebration. Bill and the kids, Jamie and Julie, had it all planned. They laughed and talked and envisioned their future together with Jana in real estate sales. As the evening wound down, Jana suddenly realized how tired she had become. The classes, studying, and exam preparation combined with the stress and anxiety of the test itself had taken its toll.

As they put the kids to bed and crawled into their own, she smiled as she closed her eyes and fell into a deep sleep. Now all she had to do was find a broker to sponsor her. Her $100,000 profession was about to begin.

Her search began the next day. Through her Sunday morning ritual of reading the paper front to back and dwelling at length on the real estate section, she was familiar with the local brokers through their advertising campaigns. She read the open house ads, the block ads, and the updates. She particularly liked reading the recognition ads acknowledging the top producers for their accomplishments. She secretly saw herself there one day among the other top agents.

She knew that with her people skills and her desire to help and serve others, she could be a very good agent. She made a list of the brokers she wanted to interview with and began making appointments that day. She weighed the pros and cons of each and went in for a second interview with three of them. By Thursday, she had a desk. She was ready to go! Two weeks of training later, she was pulling "floor duty," answering the phones and taking incoming calls from the newspaper ads. Before she knew it, she had buyers in her car looking for a home!

... **With a Single Step**

The Eppersons were a lovely young couple just getting started in their home search. After showing them several homes and finding nothing they liked, Jana set an appointment to get together again the next day and dropped them off. Over the next three weeks, Jana showed them over forty homes and finally found one that fit their criteria. After negotiating the offer and getting a signed contract, she was elated as she burst through the door with the news.

"Bill," she shrieked, "I just sold my first house!"

As they hugged each other and laughed, Bill kept saying over and over to Jana, "I'm so proud of you! I'm so proud of you!"

Jana was beaming as she went to bed. She felt like a kid on Christmas Eve. She couldn't wait until tomorrow.

Her first loan application with her first buyers! It all seemed to go by in a blur as Jana watched the buyers fill out the papers and hand the loan officer tax returns, financial reports, check stubs, and a myriad of other documents she didn't understand.

"It all looks good," the loan officer said. "We'll know more when we get the VODs and the VOEs back. I'll pull an in-file to check their FICO scores, and we'll get the GFE that shows their APR out in the mail in the next few days. Any questions?"

Not wanting to appear stupid, Jana just said, "No. You've been very helpful, thank you," and gathered up her buyers and left. As she dropped them off, she promised to stay in touch. She went home with her mind spinning and a splitting headache. "Goodness," she thought to herself, "how does anyone learn all this?"

Floor duty was more exciting than ever. "Congratulations!" her office manager said as she announced Jana's sale at the weekly office meeting. "Jana has just sold her first home!"

Everyone acknowledged her as the meeting ended, and she headed back to the phone room for her daily shift of phone duty. Anxiously, she took her seat and waited for another "good call." It didn't take long.

"I'm thinking about selling my home," the caller said, "and I would like to know what it's worth. Can you come over?" As Jana said later, "As you can imagine, I had nothing to do that night!"

She set the appointment and began to prepare for her first listing presentation!

The Dream ...

She arrived right on time and met the owners, the Mastersons. They were pleasant enough. He had been transferred to another city, and they were rather matter-of-fact about the whole thing. "It's such a shame you have to move," Jana said. "You've done such a lovely job decorating your home. It's beautiful."

"Thank you, but we're used to it," Mrs. Masterson said matter-of-factly. "This will be our fifth move in seven years. What do you think we can get for our home?"

Jana went over her market analysis, showing the Mastersons what other homes in the area sold for, what homes did not sell, and what their competition was currently in the market. As she finished, she said confidently, "So, given all that, I see your home selling in a range from $250,000 to $275,000. What do you think?"

The Mastersons looked at her, and then looked at her analysis. Then back at her. Then back at the analysis.

"But our home is much nicer than these," Mr. Masterson said slowly, his voice a little strained, as he looked again at the paperwork. "I would never sell my home for these prices. With all the improvements we've made, our home is worth more. Besides, we need to get $295,000 to make the move."

Jana listened to Mr. Masterson as he went over all the reasons the home was worth $295,000.

"Look," he said with authority that came from years of management experience, "these homes are smaller, they don't have the tile floors, the upgraded appliance package, the oversized garage, the extra attic space, the extended patio with two, TWO, ceiling fans, all the cat 5 wiring, the surround sound system, the water softener, or the trees and landscaping package. My home has to be worth more! It has more to offer!"

The silence lasted forever. Jana didn't know what to say. Her mind was reeling. She looked at the sellers, then back at her analysis. She was proud of her work. She had been so thorough, so precise. She previewed all those homes.

She had seen about thirty altogether, narrowing it down to the nine she felt were most comparable to the Mastersons' home. She knew she should say something, but she was stunned. Maybe he was right. How had she missed all that? Everything had been going so well. They seemed to like her company. It had an excellent reputation, spent a lot on advertising, had been around for quite some time, and was high profile. They seemed to like her as well. She knew her data was accurate. Yet, all of a sudden she was unsure.

Finally, Mrs. Masterson leaned over with the analysis in her hand, showing it to her husband. "Isn't that the Obersons' home?" she asked, pointing to an address on the page.

"Sure is," he said and then looked at Jana. "We know that home. It sold for more than that."

Now she was reeling. She didn't know what to say.

"How many homes have you sold in this area?" he asked her.

"N-n-none," Jana muttered, wishing she were somewhere else. She had never felt so attacked or at a loss for words in her entire life.

"Well," Mr. Masterson finally said, "we certainly do appreciate all your hard work and your time. We'll think about it and let you know."

Jana had a knot in her stomach. She knew she should say something in her defense, but she didn't know what. "Okay," she managed to reply. "Let me know." With that, she gathered up her things and was escorted to the door.

Suddenly, it was over. As she drove home, she replayed the evening over and over in her mind, trying to get through the confusion and frustration she felt. She ran the gamut of emotions, from being proud of herself for having the courage to face the unknown of her first listing presentation to massive doubt about herself and her abilities because she hadn't known how to address the Mastersons' concerns. She grew angry as she recalled seeing herself sitting there with nothing to say, a stunned mullet gaping as though it were feeding on bugs on the surface of a stagnant pond. She was so preoccupied with her thoughts that she almost ran right through the red light, smashing into crossing traffic.

"Easy," she thought. "Get a grip."

Ever the supportive one, her husband was waiting for her when she arrived home.

"How'd it go?" he asked enthusiastically.

"You don't want to know," Jana shot back as she headed to the bedroom to dress for bed.

Jana met with her office manager the very next morning.

"Shake it off," she told her. "It's a numbers game. You just need to see more people. Have you called any FSBOs? Expireds? Are you working your farm area?"

Jana hated cold calling. All her life she had been told by her parents not to talk to strangers. Now she was being told the opposite.

"Focus," her manager said. "Don't try to be everything to everybody. Just work the percentages. You can do this."

Dazed and confused, Jana headed out of the office toward the phone duty room, unsure of what to do next. Hopefully, the ads would pull.

That morning, Jana made an appointment with another buyer to show property. On her way out, her manager stopped her.

"How were the phones?" she asked.

"Good," Jana replied. "I have an appointment! I am on my way to show property right now."

"Really!" her manager responded. "What are you showing?"

Jana replied with her usual confidence, "I'm showing the Millers' place. The buyers called off the ad."

"Good," her manager said. "What else are you showing?"

Taken aback, Jana said, "That's it. That's the one they called about."

"What if they don't like it? Do you have anything else in mind? Do you know what they want? What are they looking for? How long have they been looking? When do they want to move? Are they working with anyone else? Are they qualified?"

The sudden barrage of questions left Jana dumbfounded. Once again, she was at a loss for words. Why didn't she think of those questions? Her excitement at getting a good prospect blinded her from going further. Of course she should have had a backup plan. The percentage of people who bought a home from an ad was infinitesimal, and she knew it! What was she thinking? Jana looked down at the floor, her arms full with a briefcase, binders, catalogs, and reports. She didn't know which question to answer first.

"What should I do?" she asked.

"Go," said her manager, "and call me when you're done."

Jana showed the Millers' home. The buyer wasn't that impressed. Jana went home and turned on the TV.

"Maybe I just need a break," she thought to herself.

The next thing she knew, Bill was home from work, and it was six o'clock and time for dinner. She got up just as the phone rang. It was her lender calling about the Eppersons.

"I'm afraid I've got some bad news," she said. "They don't qualify because of low FICO scores and a few charge-offs. I was hoping we could write letters or maybe get a gift, but it won't work. This deal is dead."

Bill popped in and said, "I'll fix dinner. What would you like?"

Jana hung up the phone, her heart sinking. "Nothing. I'm really not hungry, just tired. I think I'll go to bed, but thanks for asking."

Jana relayed her story to a group of other agents hanging around the coffee urn the next morning.

"Can you believe it?" she asked, still partly in shock from her conversation with the loan processor the night before. "Their credit is horrible. They couldn't qualify for a car! What makes them think they can buy a house?"

"Buyers are liars," one agent said. The others nodded in agreement, commiserating with her. "You just can't trust them."

"Yep. That's the nature of the beast," another said.

Silence set in. One by one, they drifted off, each going his or her own way. Jana was left alone with her thoughts. Now might be a good time to have that conversation with her manager.

As she knocked on the door, her manager, Joan Lewelynn, a professional, experienced, well-respected broker, waved her in as she finished her phone conversation.

"Okay, then we're on. Friday, tee time at ten o'clock. See you then."

She turned her gaze toward Jana.

"Well," she said. "What's going on in your world?"

Jana almost burst into tears. "I don't know if I can do this!" she began, fighting to gain control of the dam that was about to burst inside her. "I don't know what to do! None of the things I've run into were covered in my real estate classes! My deal with the Eppersons is dead—they have bad credit. The listing presentation I went on was horrible. They acted like I had no integrity, like I was trying to under-price their home to sell fast just so I could get a quick commission. I've never felt so humiliated in my life! I just don't think I'm cut out for this!" Tears rolled down Jana's cheeks.

Joan had seen it all before. Innocent and new to the world of marketing, sales, and negotiations, Jana was going through the typical transition period from employee to businessperson. Only time would tell if she would survive.

As Jana sobbed and vented her frustrations about the business, Joan's mind drifted. She had heard this story dozens of times in her career as a manager. The faccs and the names changed, but the story was the same. The frustration was always the same. The illusions, the heartaches, the confusion, the situations, and the predicaments were all the same. She watched Jana and nodded occasionally, but her mind was elsewhere.

"Good gosh," she thought, "I've recruited another one. She'll never make it if she doesn't get with it. I wish the schools that taught these new agents would do a better job of preparing them. Don't they know there is more to this business than a license?"

Jana was looking at her as if waiting for some sort of a response.

"Look," Joan said, not at all concerned that she had been caught daydreaming while Jana was sharing her heart. "Just go out there and make more appointments. Remember, it's a numbers game. Your income is in direct proportion to the number of appointments you have. You just need to see more people. You'll be fine. How many appointments do you have lined up this week?"

"None," Jana said cautiously, recoiling at the thought. "And after these past two, I may not want another one," she thought to herself.

"You have to fill up your pipeline," Joan told her. "You put a lot in, and a little comes out the other end. Keep going! You're doing great! That's just the way the business is. It will come around if you just keep doing what you're doing. Believe me; I've been there. I know how you feel. You're a good agent, and you'll do well. Just keep going." Encouraged by her kind words, Jana vowed to get back at it.

"Two transactions don't make a career," Joan told her. "Good or bad, you just need to do more deals." With that in mind, Jana went in for her phone duty shift, fired up and with a new attitude.

... Becomes a Nightmare

Soon the phone was ringing again.

"Yes," the caller said, "I'm calling about the ad in the paper 'Room to Roam,' and I was wondering if I could ask you a few questions?"

With that, she was off again, and in no time at all, she had the Smiths out in her car showing them homes. They didn't find anything they particularly liked, but agreed to get together the next day. Jana worked with them over the next three months. She showed them home after home. Every home she showed had something wrong with it—too big, too small, too many rooms, or not enough rooms. Exasperated and tired, they continued their search. In between showings, she had a listing presentation to do that day.

She listed the Harrelsons' home that evening and was out showing the next afternoon until dark, still unable to find the Smiths a home that met their seemingly impossible criteria.

Mr. Harrelson called. "Are you holding our home open this weekend?" he asked.

Taken by surprise, Jana said, not wanting to upset her brand-new clients and her only listing, "Uh, well, sure, if that's what you want. I guess I could do it from 1 to 4."

"Great," Mr. Harrelson said, sounding pleased. "We will see you then."

Jana shopped the Smiths all day Saturday to no avail and made an appointment to meet with them again Monday afternoon. The Sunday open house was rather slow, with only two couples coming through, both neighbors. She called the Smiths that night to confirm their Monday appointment.

"I'm glad you called," Mrs. Smith said. "I was just about to call you and cancel."

"Really? Why?" Jana asked.

"Well," she said, "we went to a new subdivision today and bought a home, but thanks for all your work."

The air left Jana's lungs as if she had been kicked in the stomach. Stunned, she thought, "I can't be hearing what I'm hearing." Finally, after several seconds, she spoke.

"What did you say?" she asked, convinced she had heard wrong.

"Well, we knew you were holding an open house, and we didn't want to waste your time, so we just went driving around. Then, we found this new house, and we fell in love with it! It's perfect for us!" Mrs. Smith said excitedly.

"How could they?" Jana thought to herself. "After all I've done for them!" She felt used, betrayed, hurt, sad, angry, disappointed, and depressed all at the same time. "I thought we were friends. I thought we had a relationship, an understanding. I thought you were working with me exclusively." These were the thoughts running through her mind, but she couldn't say them. She was too shocked. Later, after the shock would wear off, she would think of plenty to say. For now, her mind was a total blank.

She knew she had to speak, but she didn't quite know what to say. Should she express her disappointment? Should she explain to them that she is a professional on commission and that she only gets paid when something closes? Should she explain to them that she spent all those hours, gave up all those weekends with her family, gave up things she wanted to do to be with them? That being at their beck and call for months on end deserved something more than "thanks"?

Shocked and at a loss for words, Jana found herself torn and confused. She was torn because she wanted to express her disappointment at her lost time, energy, and money. She also found that she had grown fond of the Smiths and felt betrayed, as if her own husband had lied to her. How does one convey that? At the same time, she wanted to come across as a mature professional. Lastly, how could she bring herself to say these things, knowing it would dampen their enthusiasm and excitement, take away from their joy, and, in the end, only make her look worse?

Jana raised the receiver to her mouth and did the only thing she knew would be best.

"Congratulations," she said with as much emotion as she could muster. "I'm glad you found something you like."

Two weeks later, Mr. Harrelson called. "Our home hasn't sold," Mr. Harrelson began, "and you haven't even shown it yourself. We want to withdraw from our listing agreement."

That weekend, Jana went through her normal Sunday morning ritual. Coffee and paper in hand, she read from cover to cover, saving the classifieds for last. With a deep sigh, she finally picked them up. Turning to the professional section, she began looking for a job.

TESTIMONIALS

"I've found my agents' income increased when I sent them to the Psychology of Marketing course at The Austin Institute of Real Estate."
Valerie Lyday, Vice President and Branch Manager
Coldwell Banker United Realtors

✳✳✳✳✳✳✳✳✳✳✳✳✳✳✳✳✳✳✳✳✳

"Let me take this opportunity to congratulate and thank you for the great training your school is providing. Two courses presented by Wayne have been particularly helpful to my new agents. His 'How to Really Get Started in Real Estate' and 'The Psychology of Marketing' classes should be mandatory for all new agents getting into real estate. I have recently had agents take these two courses and make sales their first month in the business."
Byron Schilling
JBGoodwin Realtors
President

✳✳✳✳✳✳✳✳✳✳✳✳✳✳✳✳✳✳✳✳✳

"One advertising idea I received from the 'Psychology of Marketing' course produced over $100,000 of income to my rural development project."
Lee Hubbard
Tejas Ranch Properties

* * * * * * * * * * * * * * * * * * *

"Wayne showed me the attitude to be an outstanding person in everything I do. I earned Top Citywide and Top Statewide Remax Realtor of 2001 due to the benefits of Wayne's training."

Elizabeth Chang, Sales Agent

$15 million in volume 2001

Assisted over 700 families in listing and selling their properties

Top Citywide Remax Realtor 2001

Top Statewide Remax Realtor 2001

Received Remax Hall of Fame Award

* * * * * * * * * * * * * * * * * * *

Chapter Two
The Statistics According to NAR

How are they doing? Some statistics from the National Association of Realtors®

According to the July 2003 issue of Realtor® magazine, there were 907,738 members of the National Association of Realtors®, up from 876,195 at the end of 2002, making it the nation's largest professional trade organization. As of June 2004 there were over 1,000,000 members.

We just followed Jana through what could be classified as a new agent's typical frustrations and first encounters in the industry. Below you will read statistics provided by the National Association of Realtors®' magazine. This information came from its "Seventh Annual Income and Expense Survey" by Robert Freedman:

2001 Median Income and Expenses

Median: The point at which half the respondents reported less and half reported more.

Agents:

With 5 years experience	$20,000
With 10+ years experience	$50,000
Who work alone	$40,000
With assistants	$90,000

Age:

Under 45	$40,000
45–54	$50,000
55–64	$60,000
65+	$45,000

Region:

Northeast	$70,000
Midwest	$40,000
South	$55,000
West	$60,000

Gender:

Male	$50,500
Female	$50,000

Sources of Business:

Referrals	40%
Prospecting	33%
Open Houses	14%
For Sale Signs	11%
Advertising	2%

Effect of a Web Site:

Practitioners with a personal Web site—18.9% of respondents earn twice as much as those who don't have one.

With Web site	$90,000
Without Web site	$45,500

Expenses: Commission split

With	$45,500
Without	$66,000

Some Other Statistics

Number of Real Estate Agents in the United States: *907,738*

Average length of time in the business: *2 years*

Number of people who move each year: *42 million*

Average number of times people move in their life: *11.7*

National average for sales per year: *6 homes*

....

These statistics do not reflect the drive, desire, ability, or capability of people. It does reflect a serious flaw in how we educate and train people. Every home, club, group, or organization is a business.

Unless each one is designed, built, and run like a business, the result will look like these statistics. If agents do not design, build, and run their business like a business, they will soon be out of business. This is why we say that good grades in school do not equal success. The classes taught for obtaining a license are good for a foundation. However, once the foundation is laid, an agent who desires to become successful must begin his or her business education.

Chapter Three

The Three Steps to Getting Rich in Real Estate

Step One: Obtaining the License

Jana's story is typical of 90 percent of all new agents who enter the real estate profession. They enter the business with excitement, hope, big dreams, and high aspirations. Unfortunately, their educators and their education have failed them. Of course, Jana will be labeled the failure in this case when exactly the opposite is true. Most schools do not teach business building. They teach test passing. If the school you attend is focused only on the license and does not teach business-building courses, find another school. Quickly. The license is only step one of your career. It is merely the entry fee agents pay to get into the game. It does not provide agents with the skills necessary to compete or be successful, much less get rich.

Most of the information covered is to get the agent through the exam process and has nothing to do with the real world.

If, on the other hand, your real estate school suggested you buy this book, go right now and thank the owners as they are committed to your success.

Step Two: Building the Business

Here is the question all new agents have to ask themselves: "Do I want to be *in* the real estate business, or do I want to *own* a real estate business?" This is a business, and unless you design it and build it and run it like a business, you will soon be out of business.

This requires careful consideration as many people equate "owning a business" with "working harder than ever and having no life." They don't understand the business model. The main reason to own a business that works is so you don't have to. It's a business only if you can walk away and it continues to grow without you. Most people are very confused about this subject. They think they have to be there to run the business. The job of a business owner is not to run the business. It is to write the systems and hire people to run them. The people run the systems. The systems run the business.

That means an agent needs all the departments that exist in any business. These departments should be systemized to run automatically whether the agent is there or not. This is as simple as any franchise.

When you buy a franchise, that is what you are buying: the systems. Agents need to work **on** their business while they work **in** their business, building it with the exit in mind. Ninety percent of all businesses are a series of "replicatable events." The owner is performing the same tasks in the same way over and over again and again. These tasks can be systemized and taught to others in your growing business team.

Step Three: Investing the Profits in Low-Risk, High-Yield Investment Properties

Never before in history have so many people been blessed with so much opportunity. Is insider trading legal? It depends on what business you are in. I learned my third year that I was never going to achieve my financial goals if I kept working for commissions and, out of those, paying my broker, my expenses, and my taxes. The key to getting rich in real estate is not in listing it or selling it, but in owning it. Most of the deals I buy now never even hit the market. Brokers call me and tell me about them before they are made available to the public. Is this legal? In the stock market, no. In real estate, yes. Understanding the difference between "cash" and "cash flow" made a huge difference in my new approach to the business. I took my commissions, which were cash I received for working, and bought real estate no one else knew was for sale, thereby creating "cash flow," money that came in whether I worked or not.

This is the Three Step Success System we used to get rich. It is the same system we teach at our school and at our seminars. It is the same system we used to become rich in this business. We did it, and you can do it, too.

TESTIMONIALS

"Fantastic class! I think I learned as much in three days with Wayne as in all my time at U.T. Thanks, Wayne!"

Linda Holmbeck

"I will increase my ability to sell because of Wayne's knowledge and experience. He cared enough about me that I wanted to learn. There is really no way to put a dollar amount on how he has helped me—except for the increase in my commission check."

Dana Pope

★ ★

"Wayne is an excellent instructor that is very animated and uses many tools to encourage his students' learning process."

Lena Thompson

★ ★

"Absolutely the best class I have had anywhere."

Travis Mathews

★ ★

"I have been in the real estate field since 1977, having earned my 'stripes' in Southern California, enduring two massive down markets. During that time, I attended a host of motivational seminars and purchased truckloads of tapes and books. I soon discovered that I didn't need motivation.

"The Psychology of Marketing course is the BEST I have ever seen. It provides tools and an invaluable understanding of human nature."

Roxanne Franks

Part Two

How to Build a Business That Works ... So You Don't Have To

Chapter Four

The Purpose of the Business

Step One: Design Your Life

First, design your life. Then, design and build the business to give you that life you desire. Most people work too much. Whether they have a job or own their own business, most people work too much. It doesn't have to be that way. The most rewarding thing I have received from owning a business is the freedom it provides me. I literally do what I want to do on my own terms, every day.

Before you start denying that it could also be that way for you, let me say this: It wasn't easy, sometimes it still is not easy, and it wasn't fast. But everything I had to learn, overcome and go through to get here was worth all the aggravation, frustration and pain it took.

It began with the realization that it could be just the way I had envisioned it. I just woke up one day and decided that I was going to design my life and build the business to provide it. This was a huge shift in thinking for me because my father was the champion and prime example of hard work. Some of my earliest memories as a child were of working while my friends were playing.

My father instilled in me the value of a hard day's work. And, I have to admit, it still feels good to have created, built, planted, cleaned, polished, watered, grew, or repaired something. I worked hard all my life. I was proud of the level of work I could churn out. I could work circles around the best of them—that was my work ethic.

And where do you think all that hard work got me? It got me tired; that's where it got me.

Tired and armed with a new realization, my wife, Lynn, and I sat down and began to design our lives. We stretched our imagination. We asked ourselves what it was that we really wanted out of life. We recalled conversations with friends about the subject of lifestyle. We talked about big houses, big boats, expensive sports cars, and vacations around the world. We talked about working less while making more money and fulfilling our dreams.

Our peers looked at us like we were crazy. They did what most friends do: began to bring us "back to reality," to "the real world." In the "real world," there is either not enough time or there is not enough money. That's what kept sticking in our minds, as did what we heard all around us.

So, we quit talking to others about it, and instead, we turned to each other. We asked ourselves the question, "If time and money were not an issue, what would we do?" We then designed our lives from that perspective. Once we determined how much money our lifestyle would cost, we designed the business to provide it. Then we built the business. And now we have it—the big house overlooking the lake, just like we pictured it; the big boat, just the one we wanted; and, of course, the cars. The best part is, almost all of it is paid for either from passive income or from tax deductions, not our personal labor. Then we created another, bigger game for ourselves. I know that anyone can do what we did. It all starts with a design, a vision of what it will look like when it is built, and the faith, dedication, and persistence to build it. We figured how many months per year we were going to work, how many to travel, where we would go, what we would do, how much it would cost, and how much income we needed to generate in order to pay for it all. Then we built the business and bought the investments to pay for it all.

You will discover, as we did, that this is going to be a painful process. If there wasn't any pain, there would be no value attributed to getting through the process. If it was easy, you wouldn't like it, you wouldn't appreciate it, and you would wreck it. But, if you have clearly defined goals, a spouse or partner to share the journey with, and a well-thought-out plan, and you refuse to hear the words *no* or *quit*, you will get there.

That's why the goal-setting process is so powerful. In our case, it was about dreaming big and then having a plan to make the dreams come true.

Over the years, my wife, Lynn, and I have trained, managed, and licensed tens of thousands of real estate agents. In the following chapters, we have recapped conversations we have had with them over the years. If you are new or considering getting into the business, perhaps these conversations will answer some questions you may have. They may even answer some questions you haven't considered yet. For those of you already in the business, maybe you can relate to these conversations, and hopefully, they will provide some solutions to the two biggest problems real estate agents have: making more money and doing it in less time. The conversations are real. The names have been changed.

Lynn and I own a real estate education company, The Austin Institute of Real Estate, in Austin, Texas. We are licensed and approved by the Texas Real Estate Commission as a provider of licensure courses. We have agents approach us constantly, asking what to do to get their business off the ground.

"What do we do?" a group of students wanted to know during a break. "How do we get started?"

"You have to learn what is on the exam. Getting your license is just the first step. Once you get it, you have to then learn what you need to know in order to keep it. That's step two."

"How do we do that?" they ask.

"The business, like most businesses, is constantly changing. It's changing technically, but fundamentally it remains pretty much the same. In other words, what we did years ago we still do, but the way we do it has changed as technology has improved. You still have to plan, design, and run the business like a business, but the ways in which we do that are different."

"How so?" one asked.

"Well, although times have changed and technology has changed, we still need customers, we still need to serve those customers, and we still need to grow the business and do all the things necessary to make that happen. But the methods of acquiring and serving the customers as well as most other aspects of growing the business are very different from what they were just a few years ago. Times have changed. People have changed. Technology has changed. Rote memorization of test material is becoming less important than managing and keeping up with change. Business skills are more important than job skills. Generalization is more important than specialization."

"That doesn't sound so hard. Why do so many people quit?" a student asked.

"It's not from lack of desire, that's for sure," I told her. "Most people are very committed to real estate. It's a variety of things that causes them to leave. It's a business that looks easy to do on the outside, but once you get inside, it's not always that easy. People that do enter the business seem to make the same mistakes over and over. If you get past those, you can do very, very well. The ones who leave all seem to do the same things, and the ones who stay and succeed do the same things. If you knew what those things were, it would improve your chances of success. You would know not only what doesn't work, but what does. Most people know one or the other. Very few know both."

"Do you?" one of the students asked.

"Of course! I've been doing this for quite a few years now. I've seen them come, and I've seen them go. There is a pattern to each. Each one who leaves makes the same crucial mistakes as the person before him."

"Will you tell us what they are?" they asked, almost in unison.

"Sure," I said, looking at my watch. "You want to get together after your class?"

We agreed to meet in an empty classroom that evening. That gave me some time to think about our conversation and prepare for the next meeting. When they finished their class for the day, I was ready.

"Here," I began, "are the seven things anyone can do to build a successful business. As I said earlier today when we met out in the hallway, most people know what doesn't work, which is helpful to some extent. Knowing what to do and repeating it over and over is what brings about success. So, I will do my best to show you both. I will tell you the mistakes that are made, and what to do to avoid them or what a possible solution could be instead. To begin, how many of you have a plan?"

I was getting blank looks from every one of them.

"Plan. Do you have a business plan?" I asked again, although I already knew the answer.

"No," one of them finally answered. "I'm not starting a business. I'm just going to sell real estate."

"Decide up front: Do you want to be *in* the real estate business or *own* a real estate business? Is this going to be your hobby or your business? Either one is fine; that is the beauty of this business. You can do this business part-time and do really well.

"I have known many people over the years who have entered real estate as a second or third career after their primary career was over. They wanted to stay active, get out and meet people, learn and do new things, and sell a house or two a month. 'You can only play so much golf,' one said to me.

"Others are 'empty nesters,' folks whose children have grown up, left home, and started lives of their own, and whose spouses have good jobs. They didn't need the money; they were active and wanted something to do. If they could sell a house or two a month, buy a new car, buy a new wardrobe, and pay for an exotic vacation, they were happy.

"The real estate business is the only business I know where you can turn it on and turn it off at will, show up every now and then, and still put two, three, or four thousand dollars in the bank each month.

"However, if this is your business, you have a family counting on you, and you have bills coming due each month; therefore, you need to structure it differently. Is this going to be your business? If it is, then it needs to be designed, built, and run like a business. Most agents, when asked what they do for a living, say, 'I'm *in* the real estate business,' not 'I *own* a real estate business.'"

"What's the difference?" one asked.

"About $500,000 per year," I said.

Again, either one is fine, but if you want to work less and make more and get into the upper echelon of agents making $500,000 to $1,000,000 or more per year, this is what you do:

The Solution
Focus on What Works, Drop What Doesn't

"There are several things you need to do in order to begin designing your business," I told them. "Many questions need to be asked and answered, and many decisions will need to be made. Unfortunately, sometimes you do not have enough information in the beginning to make educated decisions. If it turns out that you have made a decision that isn't working, change it quickly. Remember, in school there is one right answer. In real life outside the classroom, it is a multiple-choice test, and you get to change your answer. Forget about being 'right' or 'wrong.' It either 'works,' or it 'doesn't work.' Focus on what works. Change what doesn't. Quickly. Most of your success will come from quickly changing from what doesn't work to what does—in other words, correcting your mistakes quickly. This business of yours is a work in progress. You are learning by trial and error. Try anything and everything. Don't worry if you've made a decision that doesn't work. I've made millions of mistakes. That's why I know so much.

Step Two: Design the Business to Give You Life

Building a real estate business is a lot like fishing. What would you do if you decided to go on a fishing trip? Plan: dates, time to leave, what to eat and drink, etc.; then prepare: gas up the truck and boat, get licenses, bait, equipment, etc.; then act: go find the fish, get them to bite, catch them, take care of them so they don't die, and so on. It's the same with a business, no matter what business it is. Most agents don't plan to fail; they just fail to plan. In order to build a house, you need a set of plans. Before risking their money, the lender is going to want to see the plans. Before beginning construction, the contractor is going to need them in order to know what you want him to build and get bids. The city wants to see them to see if they conform to the building codes. You don't want to be the only one without a plan. Once you design your life and you know how much money that will require, you can then design the business to provide you with that lifestyle.

"What is the plan for your business? Talk it over. Discuss what we just covered and tell me what you think."

They discussed this amongst themselves for a few minutes, and then a hand went up.

"Please," I said, inviting him to ask.

43

"You said we didn't have enough information to make a business plan. How do we design our business? I've never done that before and neither have the people in my group. What do we do, and what order do we do it in?"

Seven Steps to Get Started

"To start, I would focus on seven things. These seven considerations should help you design the structure of the business. There are ten crucial mistakes agents make. The first one is that they do not design the business. They have no planned method via which they are going to operate their business. There are seven things to consider in the design phase. The first one is to decide on your niche."

1. Find Your Niche

"How many licensed agents are there in the area?"

They didn't know.

\ "How many homes per month are selling?"

They didn't know.

"Currently in Austin, there are about 4,500 licensees of the local board and about 1,200 homes selling per month. When you do the math, you'll see that it is about a fourth of a house per agent. Obviously, some people are not making any money."

"How do we get our share?" Gordon asked.

"First off, you need to find a niche."

"What is a niche?" one of them asked.

"It is an untouched or untapped segment of the market. You may find it tough to be everything to everybody and work the whole town unless it is a small one. When you try to be all things to all people, you end up being no one to anyone. This is one of the most common (and fatal) mistakes small business owners and real estate agents make. 'I'm going to do it all,' they say. Sometimes you see it in advertising. 'We do it all!' they exclaim with pride. I will go into it more in detail in the marketing section, but for now just know that unless you give people a compelling reason to pick up the phone and call you, they probably won't. 'We do it all!' is not compelling and a waste of good advertising dollars.

"It is also going to be impossible for you to cover all the market segments and all the price ranges. Choose a niche and be clear about it, or you will be jumping up and running every time the phone rings.

"Here are some of the market segments. Are you going to do residential or commercial? If commercial, will you do sales or leasing? Each category has multi-family, retail, office, industrial, hospitality, etc.

If you choose residential, again, sales or leasing? Which area of town? What type of property? Multi-family, single family, condominiums, land, lots, farms, or ranches? What price range?"

According to the National Association of Realtors®, here is the breakdown on the percentage of buyers in each price range:

$0–$200,000	60%
$200,000–$400,000	28%
$400,000–$500,000	5%
$500,000 and up	12%

"The mass of the market is in the lower price ranges. If you went fishing, what would you do? Go where the fish are, correct? 'Find a need and fill it' is one of the oldest axioms of the business world. What is wanted and needed? What segment of the market is moving? Ask owners, brokers, and other top-producing agents which segments of the market are moving. Get statistics from title companies or the local Board of Realtors.

Sometimes you discover your niche after you do your market research because that research will tell you in what direction the markets are moving (so you can go there). Sometimes you decide on a niche first and then go see if there is enough business to support it. Either way is fine.

For example, you may decide to become an inner-city specialist, or focus near a local university, or specialize in lake properties, or ranches and farms. If you are from the country and have a Western liking, you probably won't be comfortable selling urban or university properties and vice versa. You already know what you like and what your natural inclinations are. However, before you build, or begin to build, a business, do the market research to determine if there is enough of a market niche there to support you."

"So, a niche is either the geographic area or price range we are going to focus on, right?"

"Exactly. It's the segment of the market you primarily work in."

2. Do Market Research

I get asked this question quite a bit. New agents want to know where to start.

"Good question," I always say, "because there is no one right answer that fits everyone. I first need to know what their experience level is, how many people they know, and how long they can go without income."

Do a Self-Analysis

"If you have no sales experience, I would suggest getting some. Leasing is a good way to do that. The commissions are smaller, but they come quicker and more often. Leasing is also great training for sales. I know some leasing agents who do quite well financially. If you lack sales experience, this would be a good way to get some since you have the opportunity to do several transactions each day.

"If you have a limited number of people in your sphere of influence, leasing may be your better option than going straight into sales. The first group of people you want to contact upon obtaining your license is going to be those in your sphere—i.e., those people who already know you. Getting strangers to do business with you is going to be harder than getting people you already know to do business with you.

"Lastly, if you can go six to eight months without income, sales might be the way to go. However, if you need income within sixty days, leasing may be the way. Even if you sold a home in the first thirty days, it is going to take about thirty more days to close. That is why your questions about sales versus leasing, geographic areas, and price ranges are good. All of this is part of your plan. If you have a sales background, a large database, and can talk to and relate to home sellers and buyers, your odds of success are better in sales. It all depends on your financial situation, your skills, and what you want to do.

"I know agents making a half-million dollars a year even though they focus on the lower end of the price range. 'Everybody who wants one should own a home,' they tell me. 'I get a lot of satisfaction using what I know to help people with less-than-perfect financial situations become homeowners.' I know other agents who would never, ever work with first-time buyers. They say it takes too long, and it's too much work getting them qualified. They prefer move-up executive buyers. They are usually more financially qualified; they have been through the process and know what to expect, and they have an excellent referral base you can tap into when you do well.

"That's why I ask, 'What do you want? What does the market want? What skills do you have? What does your research show? Where do you see your niche?'"

"Let's say I decided to stay with the lower price range. How do I know if that is a good niche?"

Ask for Help

"Once you decide on a niche, choose a title company and begin your market research. Title companies are usually happy to help you develop and grow your business. Talk to marketing representatives from two or three different companies and ask them to help you with this information in exchange for future business, then decide on one company and stay with them.

"Let's say, for example, you *are* going to focus in the lower price range because that's where most of the business is taking place (and always will). You have identified three subdivisions you think are in that range, and you have noticed for sale signs going up and coming down frequently. The homes are nice, the schools are good, the location is convenient, and the homes seem to sell without sitting for a long time. Ask the title company how often they turn over. In other words, if the subdivision has nine hundred homes, how many sell in a year? The title company can tell you. This will tell you the size of that market niche you are researching. The report may look something like this: three hundred of the residents have been there less than two years, four hundred between three and seven years, and two hundred of them longer than seven years. What does this mean? People move on average every five to seven years. So, the three hundred who have been there less than two years aren't moving—they just got there. The ones over seven years are probably there to stay. That leaves four hundred candidates. Not bad. Part of your preparation would be to create a newsletter that you could send to these four hundred on a monthly basis.

If you list 5 percent, that's twenty homes. Let's say you list them and another agent sells them, so you are receiving the listing commission. If you list them for 7 percent commission, and the average price is $225,000, and you are on a 50/50 split with your broker, you will earn $78,750.

Drive the area. Become an expert. Where are the schools, shopping venues, religious centers, daycare providers, employers, entertainment areas, movies, restaurants, plays, theaters, sports facilities, and any and all items of interest? Start small in one area and drive in ever-increasing concentric circles, expanding your knowledge base. Learn where things are and how to get there. Be informed and informative. How many homes are on the market? How many in your price range? In your geographic area? How many are selling? What price ranges are selling? How long are they on the market before they sell? What, if any, concessions are sellers having to make? How many months of inventory does your market have? Your credibility with both sellers and buyers increases if you can articulate what is happening in the marketplace."

I paused and then said, "That was a lot of information. Any questions?"

"Yes," said Bill. "What do we do when we find all that information?"

"Good question. Part of being a successful businessperson is being able to identify what information is important. Now that you have your license, it is time to get on with part two of your business, which is keeping it. There is a lot of information out there. You need to know what is relevant and what isn't," I explained.

Three Reasons to Know This

"The first reason for analyzing the statistics is to determine if this area provides enough activity to support you. Go where the fish are. Focus on areas with high turnover. Just because you think the area might be good, does not mean it will be. Your gathering and analysis of sales activity will allow you to determine via statistics whether or not you want to focus your time, money, and energy here. That's the first thing to determine; is there enough activity to support me?

The second reason you want to gather this data is to be able to use it when you are representing a seller in a transaction.

Let's say the couple that calls from your direct mail piece is considering selling and wants you to tell them what their home is worth. Is that all they want to know? Of course not. If that was all there was to it, you could just call them back and say, 'It's worth between $150,000 and $170,000.' What they are really saying is, 'We're thinking about selling, and if we can get enough money out of our home to make the move, and we find a competent real estate agent we like and trust, we will probably move.'

"They don't just want to know the price. They want to know if you are capable of representing them, and if so, how you would do it. They want to know how knowledgeable you are.

"Knowing how many businesses are moving in, how many jobs are projected to be created, how many homes are being absorbed, and how you intend to attract those buyers to this house is what they want to know, always keeping in mind that you are probably not the only agent they are talking to. That's why you need this information so that you can professionally advise them.

"Here is how you analyze the data. Find the total number of homes on the market. Let's say it's 5,000. Now find how many have sold year-to-date. Divide the number sold by the number of months just ended, and you know how many are selling each month. If it is March, and there have been 2,000 sales, there are 1,000 sales per month for the months of January and February. If it's July, and 6,000 homes have sold from January through June, there are 1,000 sales per month. If it's November, and 10,000 homes have sold from January through October, there are 1,000 sales per month. Now you know how many are selling each month. Divide the number of homes on the market (5,000) by the number of sales per month (1,000). That gives the number of months of inventory. If, in your area, you have 5,000 homes on the market, and 1,000 are selling per month, then you have a five-month supply.

You can narrow or widen this search to include or exclude any factor you want. You can go macro or micro. You may want to get more specific or you may want to get more general.

You can pull the same data for just that subdivision, or just one-story homes, or two-story homes, or a particular price range (for example, $125,000–$175,000 or $500,000–$700,000).

What do the sellers want to know? How long will the home be on the market before it sells? How much will it sell for? Can you sell it? Why should they hire you?

Statistical data from your local Multiple Listing Service will show them what they can reasonably expect from the market. The market is determined by buyers, not sellers. This data will show what buyers are buying and how long it takes for homes to sell as well as the price range their home should sell in. Your ability to show, interpret, and explain the data will determine the correct price range.

The other reason to study statistical data is to learn to spot trends as they occur in the marketplace. Is the market good or bad? Neither. It just depends. There is never a bad real estate market. It's either good for sellers or good for buyers. When someone asks me how the real estate market is doing, I say, 'If you're buying, it's great!' or I say, 'If you're selling, it's great!' depending on whether we are in a buyers' market or a sellers' market. Statistics tell me whether the market is moving in the direction of the buyer or the seller, or if it is just stagnant. Generally speaking, it is a buyers' market when inventory levels are eight to ten months or more.

"This means there is more supply and less demand, causing prices to fall and sellers to make more concessions in order to sell their homes. When inventory levels are six to eight months, the market has achieved equilibrium. Less than six months' inventory becomes a sellers' market. A sellers' market occurs when supply, or the number of available homes, is low and demand is high, causing homes to sell quicker and often for more money. When talking to sellers about marketing their home, find out which type of market currently exists."

"Okay," said Bill. "That makes sense. Basically, there are three reasons why I need to do my market research. I need to know if the niche I have chosen to focus on has enough activity in it to support me, right?"

"Exactly. Lots of agents flock to the higher-end homes when the economy gets good. However, when the economy turns down, the high-priced homes are the first to slow down sales-wise. That niche becomes crowded, more homes come on the market, fewer homes sell, inventory levels climb, demand falls, and there aren't enough sales to support all the agents in that niche. That's when you have to reinvent yourself and go find a new niche quickly. Otherwise, you may not survive. It's like having the only pizza place next to the biggest high school. Then there are two. Then five. The niche fills with competitors. Then school lets out for the summer. Then demand falls.

"Then they don't make any money because they get into a price war, fighting for a shrinking customer base instead of finding a new niche. As a businessperson, you have to constantly be monitoring the market so you can predict the changes before they occur."

Bill responded, "I got it. The second reason is to learn to analyze the data so I can advise my clients as far as a marketing plan, depending on what is happening in the marketplace."

"That's it." I continued, "That data combined with what the sellers' goals are. It's not just the market conditions, although market conditions are important to know. You also need to know what the seller wants to achieve. Sometimes the shift from a sellers' market to a buyers' market can be sudden, maybe a matter of months.

"Builders have started building homes in a sellers' market and, by the time the homes were finished, ended up in a buyers' market. That's how fast it can change. Or, buyers may buy a home in a sellers' market, paying top dollar, then decide to sell and move when the economy turns down just a year or so later. They are not very happy when you tell them that their home is worth less than they paid for it just a few months earlier. That's why you need the statistics, not just your opinion.

"You also have to find out why the sellers want to sell. Some may be in financial straits and need to get out of the home quickly. Some can take their time, and if the home sells, great, and if it doesn't, they don't care. Some homes need some cosmetic updating before being placed on the market, and some look like a new model. If you are in a buyers' market, the sellers have to sell quickly, and the home needs work, you are looking at a rather large price reduction in order to get it sold. However, if the home is in pristine condition, it's a sellers' market, and they have time, they will probably get more for their home."

Therefore, it is a combination of factors that make the difference between the average agent and the top producers:

- The ability to ask good questions and discover the client's wants and needs.
- The ability to analyze the market.
- The ability to advise each client individually and independently.

"The third reason is so I can learn to spot the trend?"

"Yes," I answered. "Learning how to identify a changing market before or as it is changing will make all the difference. The marketing plan for a home when it is a sellers' market is very different from the marketing used in a buyers' market.

"Also, you may want to change your niche. If you are in the high end and the economy goes south, go with it. Drop to the lower levels until it comes back. Maybe shift from representing sellers to representing buyers. If you are in the lower range, maybe begin working with investors. They come out of the woodwork when the economy gets bad. Like I said, what is bad for some is good for others. What is good for some is bad for others. It's never a 'bad' real estate market for everyone. Someone is always benefiting."

"Wow." Bill whistled. "I never knew that the market research would play such an important role in the design of the business."

"I understand," I told him. "Just because you *think* there is a market for your product or service does not mean that there *actually is* a market. Millions, even billions, have been lost by business owners overestimating the size of the market. Sometimes, even when the research shows that there is a strong market, it can disappear in an economic downturn. That's why you have to be flexible, keep watching the market and gathering and analyzing statistics, and be able to reinvent yourself. Not every idea is a good idea."

"Is that why you said what you said in class?" Bill asked.

"What was that?"

"Every problem begins with a good idea." We both laughed.

3. Capital

"How much income am I going to need to get started?" Sally asked.

"Do you have savings? A line of credit? Borrowing capacity?

"Approximately 1,000,000 new businesses are started in this country each year. Within the first five years, approximately 80 percent fail, mainly because they are undercapitalized.

"Thousands of new agents enter the business each year. Most leave in the first year mainly because they are undercapitalized.

"Having a good product or service alone will not make you successful. You will need enough capital to sustain the marketing plan and the other ongoing business expenses until customers begin to buy what you are selling. How much capital will you need? Your budget will give you an idea."

4. The Budget

The following is a list of typical start-up fees to get started in the real estate business. Check with a local broker, Board of Realtors®, or your local real estate school to determine any additional fees you might incur getting started in the business.

CHECKLIST FOR REAL ESTATE
START-UP FEES

❑   Licensing Courses

Tuition Total   _____

Books Total   _____

❑   State application fee   _____

❑   State examination fee   _____

Total   _____

Once you become licensed, you may incur the following fees:

❑   Local Board of Realtors® MLS dues   _____

❑   Local Board of Realtors® Orientation fee   _____

❑   Annual dues (often prorated)   _____

❑   Lock box key/Palm Pilot (for access to listed property)   _____

❑   Multiple Listing Service fee   _____

❑   Business cards   _____

❑   Personal name ryder signs   _____

❑   For Sale/Sold signs   _____

❑   Lockboxes (to place on properties you list) #_____

@$_____ea.   _____

CHECKLIST FOR REAL ESTATE
START-UP FEES (continued)

❑   Training fees   _____

❑   Announcements   _____

❑   Web site development   _____

❑   Autoresponder   _____

❑   Just Listed/Just Sold cards   _____

❑   Office supplies   _____

❑   Briefcase   _____

❑   Wardrobe   _____

❑   Automobile   _____

Total: _____

Next, fill out an income statement. An income statement lists all the income and expenses the business will incur. One thing new agents underestimate is the cost of running their business. Sit down, think, and make some projections. Ask the brokers you interview. Ask agents who are already in the business. What is it going to cost to operate your business on a monthly basis? Where is that income going to come from: borrowing or savings, or does it have to be generated by sales? The main thing is to know how much money you will be spending every month. This is your budget. Put yourself down as an expense (see sample below, "Salaries—officers"). You become an employee of your own company. I suggest incorporating. This is your business, called You, Inc. It doesn't cost that much to incorporate, and it is easier to organize, track, and run. Corporate entities and structure is a big subject. This is where a good lawyer comes in handy. I recommend a simple "C" corporation.

You will have two sets of numbers on your budget: projected and actual. Each month, sit down and compare these two. In the beginning, you are estimating how much it will cost to operate your business each month. At the end of the month, the guesswork will be done. Now you know. Compare these numbers month to month, both projected and actual. Then keep your eye on them. If something gets out of line and expenses begin to rise without a corresponding rise in sales (or other income), you could very easily find yourself in a cash crunch. If you have no money, it doesn't matter how you budget.

However, once you start making more than you need, the budget acts as a brake to keep you from spending it.

At first, it is mainly guesswork. At the end of the first year, you will have twelve months of history, so the second year will be more accurate. By the third year, you will know exactly what percent of revenue each expense represents, which allows you to monitor the business better. For example, if marketing is 20 percent of revenue, and it goes to 30 percent with no increase in sales, something is wrong.

If office supplies are running 15 percent, and it jumps to 25 percent with no increase in sales, something is wrong. I like to monitor this data monthly so I can catch increases and discrepancies early in the game. See the example on the following pages.

YOU, Inc.
Statements of Revenue and Expenses—
Income Tax Basis
Year ended December 31, 200_

REVENUES	Projected	%	Actual	%
Listing Income				
Resale homes	_____	_____	_____	_____
New homes	_____	_____	_____	_____
Other	_____	_____	_____	_____
Total Listing Income	_____	_____	_____	_____
Sales Income				
Resale homes	_____	_____	_____	_____
New homes	_____	_____	_____	_____
Other	_____	_____	_____	_____
Total Sales Income	_____	_____	_____	_____
Total Revenue	_____	_____	_____	_____
COST OF REVENUES				
Commissions Paid				
Listing agent	_____	_____	_____	_____
Buyer's agent	_____	_____	_____	_____
Referral fees	_____	_____	_____	_____
Other	_____	_____	_____	_____

	Projected	%	Actual	%
Total Cost of Revenue	_____	____	_____	_____
Gross Profit	_____	____	_____	_____

OPERATING EXPENSES

Accounting	_____	____	_____	_____
Advertising	_____	____	_____	_____
Auto expense	_____	____	_____	_____
Bad checks	_____	____	_____	_____
Bank service charges	_____	____	_____	_____
Board dues	_____	____	_____	_____
Brochures	_____	____	_____	_____
Business cards	_____	____	_____	_____
Business gifts	_____	____	_____	_____
Computer expense	_____	____	_____	_____
Continuing education	_____	____	_____	_____
Contract labor	_____	____	_____	_____
Contributions	_____	____	_____	_____
Copies	_____	____	_____	_____
Depreciation expense	_____	____	_____	_____
Dues and subscriptions	_____	____	_____	_____
Equipment lease	_____	____	_____	_____
Insurance—life	_____	____	_____	_____
Insurance—health	_____	____	_____	_____
Internet and Web expense	_____	____	_____	_____
Legal and professional	_____	____	_____	_____

	Projected	%	Actual	%
Marketing and promotion	_____	____	_____	_____
Meals and entertainment	_____	____	_____	_____
MLS dues	_____	____	_____	_____
Office supplies	_____	____	_____	_____
Postcards	_____	____	_____	_____
Postage and delivery	_____	____	_____	_____
Printing and stationery	_____	____	_____	_____
Referral fees	_____	____	_____	_____
Rent	_____	____	_____	_____
Repairs and maintenance	_____	____	_____	_____
Salaries—employees	_____	____	_____	_____
Salaries—officers	_____	____	_____	_____
Signage	_____	____	_____	_____
Taxes	_____	____	_____	_____
Telephone	_____	____	_____	_____
Travel	_____	____	_____	_____
Utilities	_____	____	_____	_____
Total Operating Expenses	_____	____	_____	_____
Net Ordinary Income (Loss)	_____	____	_____	_____

OTHER INCOME

Referral income	_____	____	_____	_____
_____	_____	____	_____	_____
_____	_____	____	_____	_____
Total Other Income	_____	____	_____	_____

	Projected	%	Actual	%
Net Income (loss) before Federal Income Tax	_____	_____	_____	_____
Federal Income Tax	_____	_____	_____	_____
NET INCOME (LOSS)	_____	_____	_____	_____

5. Bookkeeping

"How do I set up my books?" George asked. "Is there any special or particular method that is better than another?"

"Yes." I advised him, "Set up a separate bank account and put your seed capital in that account and set up your bookkeeping system. Find a CPA and have a conversation with him about the best way to keep a set of books. What expenses are deductible? How do you keep track of them? Get away from paper if possible. QuickBooks is an excellent program for small businesses.

If you have credit cards, see if you can get one issued in the name of your company. Use personal cards and personal checks for non-tax-deductible purchases and the company card and company checks for tax deductible purchases. For example, your dry cleaning bill may be above average. Unfortunately, the IRS will not allow you to deduct dry cleaning services from your income taxes, so pay that with a personal check. When your vehicle needs tires, pay that with a company check, as automobile repairs and maintenance *are* deductible expenses. The car can be in your name. It doesn't have to be in the name of the corporation for you to deduct the payments and expenses. If you can't get separate credit cards, use one checkbook for personal purchases and one for business purchases.

Keep the receipts separate and code the checks **when you write them.** It is very difficult to go back and recreate what checks were for what expenses at tax preparation time. Get in the habit of noting on the check what that check is for. Your CPA can provide you with the codes, called a Chart of Accounts (see the example below). Rather than write the check and hope the bookkeeper understands or knows what it is for, code the check accurately in order to eliminate all doubt. Tires are an auto expense. Auto expense is code 6072. Just write 6072 on the check, and your bookkeeper can do his or her job without having to track you down and ask you about each specific purchase or payment. Obviously, tires would be an auto expense, but sometimes what you bought and the purpose it serves are not so obvious to others, so make it easy. Set up a system and teach people how to use it effectively and efficiently.

Keep focusing on eliminating yourself from the business by writing and refining your systems. Work on the business while you work in it. If you have a bookkeeper who can't do her job because she doesn't know how to classify an expense and has to stop what she is doing in order to track you down and ask you to remember what the check is for, you do not have a system. You should be making sales and not answering such questions. If you are answering such questions, then you'll find that you have a huge problem on your hands.

When you are small and just starting out, this little phone call is no big deal, but when you grow your company and you have many clients and many things happening simultaneously, this becomes an irritating, time-wasting, annoying event. It won't just be about one check or a check here and there. It will be about this little detail or that little detail, or this client or that client, or this closing or that closing, and pretty soon, the whole business grinds to a halt. No sales are being made, and no money is being generated because you tried to remember to do everything, and no one can do his or her job because each is dependent on you. Start off on the right foot. Systemize everything as you go along. By 'systemize it,' I mean write down what it is you do step-by-step.

Make it so that anyone can read what you wrote and do the task without asking you how it is done. Do this with every aspect of the business. You should plan on getting out of the business, at least the administrative side of it, as soon as possible. If you cannot hire a bookkeeper in the beginning, make it a goal to do so ASAP. You can't make money while sitting behind a desk or if everything is left up to you."

EXAMPLE: *CHART OF ACCOUNTS*

INCOME

Listing income

1020-Resale homes

1022-New homes

1023-Other

Sales income

1030-Resale homes

1031-New homes

1033-Other

EXPENSES

6010-Accounting

6020-Advertising

6066-Auto, fuel

6072-Auto, repair and maintenance

6080-Bad checks

6085-Bank charges

6090-Board dues

6095-Brochures

6100-Brokerage supplies

6105-Brokerage marketing

6112-Business cards

6113-Business gifts

6115-Computer expense

6120-Continuing education

6123-Contract labor

6125-Contributions

6130-Copies

EXPENSES (continued)

6132-Depreciation expense

6135-Dues and publications

6140-Equipment lease

6160-Insurance, auto

6162-Insurance, business

6185-Insurance, health

6196-Internet and Web expense

6200-Legal and professional

6205-Marketing and promotion

6210-Meals and entertainment

6215-MLS dues

6220-Office supplies

6250-Postcards

6280-Postage and delivery

6300-Printing and stationery

6340-Rent

6350-Repair and maintenance

6357-Referral fee

6360-Salary, employee

6361-Salary, bonus

6380-Salary, office

6390-Signage

6440-Tax, payroll

6460-Telephone

6470-Travel

6480-Utilities

6. Accounting

"I don't need a CPA. I do my own taxes."

I hear this every now and then, and my response is always the same: "I don't fix my own car, I don't cut my own hair, I don't dry clean my own clothes, and I am not about to do my own taxes."

Why? Simple, I don't know all the tax codes.

I will go into this more in chapter ten, but for now I will say this: My job is to grow the business, not become a tax expert. I hire a bookkeeper to organize the accounts and a CPA to assimilate the information, prepare the returns, make sure all the deductions I am allowed by law to take are taken, keep me in compliance, and advise me on how to prepare for the future.

Jimmy asked, "Why do you need both? Aren't they the same? What's the difference?"

"Bookkeeping and accounting are not the same. Your financial statement is comprised of two parts: income statement and balance sheet.

Each of these also has two parts. The income statement is comprised of the income and expenses of the individual or business (it can be, and should be, done on each—i.e., you will have one financial statement for yourself and one for the corporation). The balance sheet consists of assets and liabilities.

Bookkeeping is the accumulation and record-keeping part of the financial section of your business. It is the income statement, which consists of income and expenses. Accounting is the assimilation of the income statement and all the assets and liabilities together to form a financial statement, which is a snapshot in time of how the business is performing (see sample Balance Sheet below). An accountant can perform bookkeeping functions, but a bookkeeper cannot perform accounting functions.

Accountants and CPAs must be licensed; bookkeepers need not be. My bookkeeper comes in weekly for two days and does all the bookkeeping functions. This information then goes to the accountants, who generate a report monthly. Every month I receive a report on the financial condition of the company. This tells me what areas are performing well and which areas are not and should be addressed. I also know how much money was spent on each expense and the result of the expenditure by looking at the income statement.

The financial statement is the report card for your business. It tells you how well you have mastered the subject."

YOU, Inc.
Statements of Assets, Liabilities, and Equity—Income Tax Basis
Year ended December 31, 200_

ASSETS   (CURRENT YEAR)

CURRENT ASSETS

    Cash in bank   _____

    Accounts receivable   _____

    Prepaid federal tax   _____

    Accounts receivable, officers   _____

    Accounts receivable, others   _____

    Total Current Assets   _____

FIXED ASSETS

    Furniture and fixtures   _____

    Machinery and equipment   _____

    Automobiles   _____

    Leasehold improvements   _____

    Accumulated depreciation   _____

    Total Fixed Assets   _____

OTHER ASSETS

      Organization costs   _____

      Accumulated amortization   _____

      Security deposits   _____

      Cash value of life insurance   _____

      Total Other Assets   _____

TOTAL ASSETS   _____

LIABILITIES & EQUITY   (CURRENT YEAR)

CURRENT LIABILITIES

      Accounts payable   _____

      Credit cards payable   _____

      Contract labor payable   _____

      Payroll liabilities   _____

      Sales tax payable   _____

      SEP payable   _____

      Federal income tax payable   _____

      Deposits held   _____

      Current portion of long-term debt _____

      Total Current Liabilities   _____

LONG-TERM DEBT, less current portion   _____

TOTAL LIABILITIES   _____

EQUITY

    Common stock   _____

    Additional paid in capital   _____

    Retained earnings   _____

    Net income (loss)   _____

    Total Equity   _____

TOTAL LIABILITIES & EQUITY   _____

7. Scheduling

"Okay," said Gordon, "I've found my niche, done my market research, I have enough savings to get me through the first year, I know my budget, and I have a bookkeeper and an accountant. What do I do to generate some business?"

"Now that you've chosen your niche, have your budget projections, know your monthly expenditures, have secured enough capital to keep you going, and know how to handle the money when it comes in, it is time to focus on generating that income. If you are coming from an employee environment where your time was arranged for you, you are now the one responsible for arranging your time in your new real estate business. Time and money are the two most valuable assets you have, and the success of your business is dependent on how you spend them.

You may find your schedule is the opposite of what it used to be. Most people work during the weekdays; so, whether they are selling or buying, the process of listing their home for sale or having the time to look for a new one to buy usually occurs in the evenings or on the weekends. If you are going to fish where the fish are, this is when you will be doing most of your work. Once the basic structure is in place, it is time to focus on generating leads and income. I call these activities income-producing activities, or IPAs for short.

Some agents say, 'I just won't work weekends. If buyers or sellers are serious, they will arrange to get off work and meet me on my schedule.' Nonsense.

Not many people can go to the boss and say, 'Hold all my calls for the next three hours. I will be in the conference room interviewing real estate agents. One is coming over to give me a listing presentation,' or, 'I am thinking about moving, maybe buying a new house. I won't be in this week because I am going house hunting, and my real estate agent doesn't work weekends.' At most places, that approach won't go over very well. People can be very serious about moving, but they are just as serious about keeping that job that helps them pay for the house you are helping them find. Is making the customer work on your schedule in the best interests of the customer? Are you really going to say, 'Look, I know how badly you want to move into the $400,000 range, and I also know that your company is in the process of introducing a new product and needs you there to launch it and so you are only available to look for homes on the weekend, but I don't work weekends. If you are serious about moving, you will have to take off work'? Of course you are not going to say that.

Instead, you are going to meet with them, interview them, provide them with world-class service, explain how you operate, get an agreement, and turn this couple into fanatical customers who will sing your praises to anyone and everyone they meet.

They are going to open up their sphere of influence to you and become a referral stream that has a lifetime value of several tens of thousands of dollars."

Focus on Income-Producing Activities

Your number one priority is setting appointments. Your income is in direct proportion to the number of appointments you have per week. Of all the jobs there are to do in your business, making appointments is number one. *You are in the lead-generation and education business.* Without sales, it doesn't matter how good the rest of your organization functions. Get a 3 x 5 card and write this question on it: How many hours per day do I spend on income-producing activities? Put that in a place like the bathroom mirror where you can see it first thing every day. Keep asking that question to yourself over and over. Fill your schedule with as many IPAs as possible, particularly evenings and weekends.

You are either on an appointment or doing something to generate a new one. I don't spend much time on things that don't make money. I focus on IPAs every day and leverage the rest of my tasks out to someone else. That is the whole idea of having a team. My wife, Lynn, holds down the fort and manages the staff while I continue to search for more opportunities to increase our income. She, in turn, has a staff and a personal assistant to assist her in running the business and the real estate.

She handles day-to-day operations, interacting with the customers, the bookkeeper, the CPA, the attorneys, the tenants, and the vendors. She handles the "inside" operations while I go "outside" and focus on increasing our income through expanding the business and finding real estate investments. I spend 95 percent or more of my time on IPAs. This is something you will spend more and more time on as your business grows and as you add administrative staff to assist you in staying out of the office.

IPAs versus Admin.

Here is a list of income-producing activities and administrative tasks. Your focus needs to be on IPAs.

IPAs:

Listing presentation

Preparing   CMA
(comparative market analysis)

Answering correspondence

Open house

Shopping buyers

Previewing property

All other marketing activities

Cold calling

Door-knocking

Networking

Phone opportunity

Admin.:

Bookkeeping

Filing

Follow-up with clients

Ordering supplies

Handling mail

Accounts payable

Accounts receivable

Closing transactions

Progress, Not Perfection

We all begin at the same place, so remember, it's progress, not perfection. Some people get frustrated when progress doesn't come fast enough. That is why a plan is so important. It gets and keeps you on track while tracking your progress. It's where you end up that matters. I want to end up free from the chores I dislike, and doing what I enjoy every day. Bless the team!

Sample Schedule

Below is a recommended schedule. You will make some adjustments to fit your own situation.

Sunday:

Noon—church or time with family

1:00–6:00 PM—hold open house, buyers in your car showing property, call on For Sale By Owners

7:00–9:00 PM—Make appointments for the rest of the week

Monday:

10:00 AM—read, study, exercise, etc.

10:00 AM–12:00—make lunch appointments for the rest of the week

12:00–1:00 PM—lunch with prospect, customer, someone who will do business with you or refer business to you (do not go to lunch with other agents—they will not buy or sell—make it a business lunch)

1:00–3:00 PM—property preview; go see all properties and new MLS listings; see all listings in your primary service area (PSA)

3:00–6:00 PM—phone/floor opportunity or market analysis in preparation for listing presentation

6:00–9:00 PM—listing presentation or making appointments

Tuesday:

Same schedule

Wednesday:

Same schedule

Thursday:

OFF

Friday:

Work ON the business. Prepare to get out of the business. Write or refine systems, implement new strategies, improve and automate lead generation, follow up on referral generating systems.

Every part of your business that is repetitive is duplicatable. Whatever you do over and over, write a system that describes how to do it and hire someone else to do it. What do you pay someone to do your administrative tasks? Ten dollars an hour? So, when you do the administrative tasks, what are you paying yourself? Ten dollars an hour!

Saturday: OFF/Time with family

That's the recommended schedule: work four days **in** the business, one day **on** it, two days off. Obviously, this schedule is an ideal schedule. It is something to work toward. As I've said, you must accommodate your client's schedule. One key in this business is to remain flexible and to constantly prioritize.

I looked over at Gordon. "Does that help?"

"Sure. It's just that I came from a structured environment. My time was scheduled for me. I'm really not sure what I need to do to produce the best results and be the most efficient and effective."

Seven Time Management Tips

1. Keep a calendar of what you do hour by hour for two weeks straight without fail. If you find yourself wondering where your time went, this will tell you. Every time you find yourself short on time, do this

exercise. It will tell you where you spent your time. Time and money have a strange way of slipping away from us unless we are vigilant and accountable. Keep track of each, and you will have more of each.

2. Make a list of things to do (TTD) each day.

3. Prioritize them from most important to least important.

4. Handle each piece of paper one time. Either file it, use it, or throw it away. Don't let useless piles of paper stack up only to be thrown away later. Do it now.

5. Tackle the most dreaded tasks first.

6. Tackle the hardest ones next. Get them out of the way.

7. Spend at least thirty minutes sitting quietly and thinking. Just think.

"The design phase is often the hardest phase of the business. Creating something from nothing takes lots of drive, desire, creativity, vision, and faith. Just like designing a house, it is impossible to make every decision and anticipate every event. Some things will have to be decided on, figured out, and solved when the time comes. Start with a design, even if you scrap it all and start over again.

Your home, your school, your church, and every organization you belong to is a business. It must be designed, built, and run like a business, or it will soon be out of business. The number one mistake that new agents entering the industry make is the lack of design of their business.

This Business Blueprint form shows the different departments of your business. This will give you a visual representation of what your business will look like when it's finished. Pretend like it is already built. Start acting NOW the way you will act when it is complete. In other words, if, when it is complete, you will delegate all except the income-producing activities to someone else, begin preparing for that now. Design it that way from the beginning. How do you do that? As you master a task, write down how to accomplish that task. Write the systems as you go.

Then find someone else to run the system. Operate the business from the beginning with the mindset that you will be replacing yourself with systems.

Tip: Anytime you go below the line you are no longer the owner of your business, you are an employee.

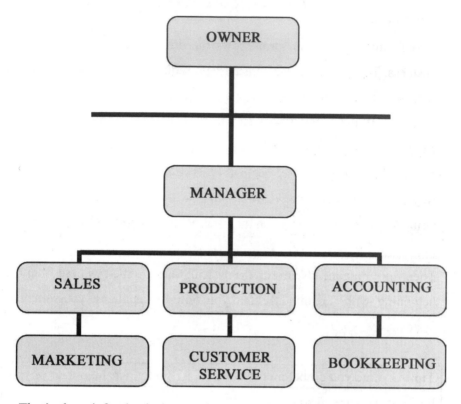

That's about it for the design portion. Now there is a skeleton, a framework, on which you can begin to hang the other pieces.

Find your niche, do your market research, set up the bookkeeping and accounting systems, create a budget, obtain the financing to run the business until it becomes self-sufficient, set the schedule, and focus on income-producing activities."

"How about this?" I asked them. "Between now and the next time we meet, decide on your niche, do your market research, and we will get into what to do to prepare yourself. Sound good?"

We agreed to meet again in a week.

To Recap:

There are seven steps to getting started with the design of your business. Before you get started, you need a plan. Design your business, build your business, and run your business like a business—without you.

Step One. Start with a niche. A niche typically is an untouched, untapped segment of the market.

Step Two. Do the market research to determine whether the niche you are going to develop is actually there, that it really does exist.

Step Three. Do you have enough capital to get your business up and running? Do you have access to capital if you need it? How much is your budget? How long can you go without income?

Step Four. Set up a budget.

Step Five. Set up the bookkeeping.

Step Six. Set up the accounting.

Step Seven. Set up your daily schedule. Immerse yourself in the environment. Get through the learning curve as fast as you can by eating, sleeping, breathing, and living it 24/7 during the first few months.

Focus on IPAs.

TESTIMONIALS

"By applying your teachings of principles of creating wealth to my real estate company, my income has consistently risen 48 percent annually. I can attest to the success of his principles and highly recommend anyone who wants to be successful in business to read what he has to say. His teachings can be a life-changing experience financially and in personal growth. Wayne is the 'guru of wealth-building.'"

Pamela Turner, GRI

Broker/CEO

"Wayne and Lynn Morgan helped me to successfully launch my real estate business through their educational and mentoring programs. Wayne's book is going to teach you how to run your business like a business, one of the key aspects of establishing a successful real estate business. In three years, I was able to reach production levels in excess of $10 million, using many of the tools and techniques I learned from Wayne's mentoring. You can do it, too!"

Debbie Espe

KW Realty

★★★★★★★★★★★★★★★★★★★★★

After 2 years of being a Realtor , with some small success under my belt, I didn t expect much from my renewal class (Psychology of Marketing). I was wrong. Great class; both informative and provocative with a dash of spirituality. What a gas! Thanks for the wake-up call."
Bobby Faas

★ ★ ★ ★ ★ ★ ★ ★ ★ ★ ★ ★ ★ ★ ★ ★ ★ ★ ★ ★

"Excellent demonstration of a new paradigm for learning."
Linda Wolf

★ ★ ★ ★ ★ ★ ★ ★ ★ ★ ★ ★ ★ ★ ★ ★ ★ ★ ★ ★

"Best class I've ever had."
Trey Freeze

Chapter Five

Proper Preparation

When I ask people why they are entering the real estate business, I hear things like, "I don't know. I like looking at houses. I think I would be good at it," or, "I have a friend in the business, and she said I would be good at it," or, "I've sold three houses, and my agent every time was not that good, but she made a lot of money, so I thought I would give it a try."

They haven't decided in which geographic area they will work, in which price range they will work, or whether they will focus on residential sales, leasing, apartment locating, commercial sales, commercial leasing, or property management. Then they get licensed, and I bump into them a few months later. I ask them the same questions, thinking that maybe, since they have had a little experience and a chance to feel their way around, they have made some decisions. They tried sales, but that didn't work, so they are now considering leasing. The truth is, they don't have a plan, they are not prepared, and they don't last long.

"Are you prepared?" I asked them at the next meeting.

"No. I haven't started. I don't have my license, and I haven't chosen a broker yet. I was waiting until I got my license," James responded.

I cringed. "Do you know what the worst four-letter word in the English language is?"

"No."

"Wait."

The Solution
Eight Things You Can Do Prior to Licensure

There are many things to do to prepare for this business, and you don't have to be in it to do them. You can do a lot of preparation prior to obtaining your license, and it makes no difference if you are going to be part-time or full-time. Some will jump into real estate with both feet, while some are planning their exit strategy from their job and will be transitioning into the business over time.

"But I don't know where to start," James replied. "I figured I would learn all that after I found a broker and got into their training program."

"I understand," I said. "All things come to those who wait, but they are the ones left behind by those who hustle. Some agents are waiting. Some are hustling."

"What would you do if you were me?" he asked.

"Here are eight things you can do to prepare for the real estate business before you ever get a license."

1. Begin Assembling Your Team

Realize that when you enter the real estate profession, you must take control of your business. You are now a CEO. This means that you don't have to know <u>EVERYTHING</u>. You don't have to do <u>EVERYTHING</u>. You must find people who are smarter than you in the different specialized areas of real estate and business. This is one of the biggest differences between the sole proprietor and the true business owner. People (your clients and customers) rely on your expertise. So, to be a true CEO of your company, you must know your strengths and weaknesses and assemble a team of experts!

There is an old story about Henry Ford, the founder of Ford Motor Company. He was on the verge of being ousted from his own company, accused of incompetence. He asked the judge to bring a telephone into the courtroom.

When it was installed and working, he invited his accusers to ask him any question about any aspect of his company. Question after question was fired at him, and time after time, Ford called the person in charge of that department, producing the answer.

You don't have to know everything. All you need to know is who to ask. You don't have to do everything. It is not your job to do it. It is your job to get it done.

By now, you have your bookkeeper, or at least a bookkeeping system that your CPA gave you. You can do without a bookkeeper in the beginning, but you will need a CPA to do your taxes, so get one early and get him or her to help you organize your books.

(Hint: Most accountants tell you what you did last year and what the consequences of that will be. Ask your accountant what to do *this* year to keep your taxes to a minimum next year. Structure it properly up front rather than recreate history.)

Hire the bookkeeper later as the growth of your business allows for it. The CPA will assist you by telling you and showing you how to prepare. Give the CPA the information to do your financial statements and tax returns. Find these professionals, interview them, explain to them what you are looking for, and hire people you can work well with.

I personally went through several accountants before I found one I could relate to and who understood me. Many are terrified of the IRS. I'm not terrified of the IRS. Do you want to know why? I don't break their rules. There are approximately 500,000 pages of tax code. Have I read those 500,000 pages? Of course not! My accountant has, on the other hand.

In those pages, it spells out which events are taxable events and which are not. A few of my previous accountants were afraid of the IRS and therefore did not take deductions that were allowed to me by law. They cost me money because they were afraid. My thought was, "If the IRS says I can deduct it, deduct it." This is a very serious subject. There is a huge difference between tax evasion and tax avoidance.

Do you know what the difference is? The difference is twenty years!

I finally found and interviewed a CPA who understood the tax code and educated me and explained to me the way certain situations allowed for certain deductions, all sanctioned by the IRS. The IRS is not the boogeyman. The IRS wants businesses to create jobs and investors to buy property. They even tell you how to do it in the tax code. It is not something to be feared. Instead, it is something else to educate yourself about so you can understand how it fits into your business and your life. I am not saying to know all of the distinctions and ramifications of the code.

What I am saying is find an accountant who does and make him or her a member of your team. My accountant is also a real estate investor. I would not have an accountant who wasn't. Because he owns his own business and invests in real estate, he knows how to advise me in structuring my business and real estate to take advantage of the deductions that are provided for in the tax code while keeping me in compliance.

The Legal Eagle

If you are in the business any length of time, you are going to have clients with legal issues you are not qualified to handle. You may have some yourself. Unfortunately, not everyone is honest. Sometimes people will take advantage of your good nature, and sometimes there are misunderstandings. Eventually you will require the services of a good attorney.

Find a local attorney who specializes in business law and/or real estate and visit with him. Introduce yourself, get his business card, tell him you are new to the business, but you are sure that your future clients will require sound legal advice. Ask if you can refer clients or call on their behalf. You are going to need legal business and real estate counsel from time to time throughout your career.

Do not leave it up to your clients to solve their own problems. If you want to get rich in this, or any other business, solve other people's problems. That's what businesspeople do. Businesspeople own the problem and solve it. If your clients could do it on their own, they wouldn't need your service.

You Get Paid for Solving Problems

Businesspeople get paid for solving problems. The bigger the problem you solve, then the bigger the check. Not everyone can successfully run a company and solve big problems. Go above and beyond the call of duty. Find a good, top-notch business/real estate attorney and be someone your clients learn to turn to when they need problems solved, advice, counsel, and results. This is another way you increase your value to the client.

Other Team Members

Here are the other members of your team you will want to look for and add as they demonstrate their professionalism and abilities to you.

Appraiser

Mortgage banker

Mortgage broker

Title company

Home inspector

Contractor

The trades:

       Electrician

       Plumber

       Roofer

       Painter

       Flooring

       A/C and heating

       Engineer

       Architect

       Foundation repair

       Interior designer/decorator

       Landscaper

       Lawn maintenance

Hint: This is what I used to tell my clients: "Over the years, I have gathered a team of professionals who assist me in providing you with the service and advice you deserve. I am going to loan them to you. They are experts in their field and will do a great job for you."

Some brokers are afraid of being sued and therefore do not refer their clients to their team of professionals who are experienced and know how to solve problems. Instead, they hand their clients a list or the Yellow Pages and have them choose one. I have had this happen several times, always with negative results. One of my listings was sold by another agent who was afraid of being sued and worked for a broker who was also afraid of being sued. The company policy, therefore, was to avoid liability altogether and to not refer anyone in case they made a mistake or did a poor job. When it came time for the inspection, the agent gave the out-of-town buyers, who were new to the city, the Yellow pages and told them to find their own home inspector. They did, and the inspector (who was also afraid of being sued) over-inspected the property. He found over $20,000 in problems to the property, and the transaction fell off. I had the property re-inspected by my inspector and had the repairs done for $2,200. The property sold shortly thereafter.

I don't know what happened to that other agent. He may be out there with those buyers to this day, going from house to house, hoping a deal comes together. Moral of the story: If they are going to sue you, they are going to sue you. You are better off referring your clients to someone you know and trust rather than hoping your clients pick the right person who is qualified. *The goal is to build a referral-based business.*

Think about it like this: You are better off referring an experienced professional that you know rather than leaving it up to your clients and hoping they find a good one. I don't want my clients to end up with a novice who wrecks the deal. I explain to my clients how the transaction will unfold chronologically, who I recommend for each step, and why I recommend that person.

By taking care of all aspects of the transaction and going above and beyond the call of duty by using the people on my team, I am able to deliver a first-class level of service, resulting in referrals. My team helps me get through closing after closing without the hiccups I see other agents have. It is very comforting (and it makes me look very good) to know that when problems arise, they are dealt with quickly. After the transaction closes, I call the members of the team and thank them. They usually thank me in return for referring them. Then I ask them for a referral. It goes something like this: Carl, just want to thank you for the great job you did on that inspection in the Smith transaction. We just came from closing, and I appreciate your help."

Carl thanks me for the job.

Then I ask, "Do you know anyone who is considering buying or selling in the next thirty days?"

Referrals are how you provide first-class service. First-class service is how you get referrals.

2. Preview Property

The second thing you can do prior to getting licensed is become familiar with property and areas. Look for areas trending. Some areas are trending up, some down. Look and you will see it. Go to as many open houses as possible. Study neighborhoods, architectural designs, price ranges, and amenities. Find out where all the schools, shopping, places of worship, parks, and clubs are located. Put yourself in the buyer's shoes. What would you be looking for if you were to move? What did you look for when you moved? Learn neighborhoods, boundaries, deed restrictions, homeowner's associations and how they operate, daycare facilities, and distances to major employers. Even after licensure, it is necessary to preview property at least two hours a day.

Knowing what is available, without having to go check the computer and look for two days, is your job as an agent. Remember, this is a business, and you must know your inventory and your market if you want to be seen as a professional.

3. Study and Learn Contracts

You will be creating legal documents without the benefit of law school. You do not need to become a lawyer to do that. Don't give legal advice. Refer your attorney to them. You do, however, need to know and understand what these forms say and mean.

Learn the basic four or five documents you will be using the most. Regardless of your state or local board affiliation, the standard list of forms will include:

- The Exclusive Right to Sell Listing Agreement
- FHA/VA Residential Contract
- Conventional Residential Contract
- Mediation Agreement
- Seller's Disclosure

Again, you don't need to become a lawyer to know and understand these forms. Study the forms to the point at which you can turn them upside down, point to the paragraph, and paraphrase it to a buyer or seller. For example, if you were taking a listing, and they were about to sign the Listing Agreement, you may say something like, "This is the legal description and street of your property. This first paragraph spells out everything you will be selling when you sell your home. Is there anything listed there that you do not want included?"

If the owner made the drapes, and they are not included, find out now before the buyer sees them and wants them. Take them down and put up replacements.

4. Learn the City

Become familiar with the big picture. People who are new to your city will want to know what it has to offer. Show the highlights of your city. Show them where they go to change their driver's license, where they go to register their vehicles, the theater district, sports facilities, lakes, beaches, and the downtown area. What new things are happening? What drives the economy? What businesses are there? What businesses are moving in? What is the political climate like? Where are the different kinds of restaurants? Your title company can be very helpful in providing you with a relocation packet or binder that shows tax rates, government offices, schools and their rankings, and a plethora of other information. On your first trip out with a buyer who is new to town, ask him if he has seen the city and if not, would he enjoy an overview before narrowing the search down to areas and specific subdivisions? Take the time to show off your city.

5. Set Up Your Web Site

You will need to have an Internet presence. Look at other agents' sites for ideas, both good and bad. You will see what works and what doesn't work.

Your site must contain five essential elements to stand any chance of success.

A. It must be easily editable.

B. It must have free reports that educate and assist the public.

C. It must have an autoresponder attached to it.

D. It must have automated home-search capability.

E. It must be easy to find.

A. It Must Be Editable

Your site will not be some stagnant event that you throw together and never touch again. It will be a dynamic, changing, moving, evolving marketing tool designed to educate prospects by providing current, valuable, up-to-date information that helps them in their buying or selling process.

As your marketing message changes week to week, your site needs to change to reflect the new message. For example, one Sunday you may run an ad that says, "Own any home on this page with zero down payment. Go to www.youragent.com for details."

They don't want to talk to you (yet). They just want the information. They don't want to be sold, they don't want to hear your sales pitch, and they don't want to go anywhere or do anything with you (yet).

Not until you have offered them something they want, given them something they want, solved their problem, addressed their concerns, heard their considerations, and established a relationship. Once you have elevated, separated, differentiated, and distinguished yourself as different from the other agents, they will contact you, talk to you, and work with you. First, there has to be a relationship. This is done by providing free valuable, relevant, pertinent information and education.

They go to your site and read your ad and your other free reports and then they call you. Therefore, you need to be able to change (edit) your site as your marketing message changes. This ad pulls well, so you decide to let it run a while. Three weeks later, calls begin to fall off, so you change it. The new ad looks something this.

Fixer-Upper

Handyman special

Bring brush, reap thousands

Desperate

www.youragent.com

You change your site again to reflect this new ad. On the home page, it says, "I have located properties in good areas that need minor repair and improvement that can be bought substantially below market value. If you are pre-approved and can move quickly, call me at 123-4567. You can also go to my reports section and download my free report, 'The 10 Reasons Every Portfolio Should Contain Rental Property.'" Just keep educating and helping them. Once they "get" that you want a relationship, not just a commission, you are on your way.

B. It Should Be Content Rich

People go where they are fed. Tell them where the food is and feed them, and they will continue to return time after time. Freely give away as much information as you can. Information is to be shared, not hoarded. The more information you give freely without cost or any obligation, the more you will be seen as the expert. If you don't tell them anything, they will think you don't know anything. Tell them as much as you can, and they will think you know an awful lot.

Some may take your information and sell their home without you. That could happen. Others will say or think, "Wow. There is a lot to this home-selling process. I never thought of some of these things. Maybe he or she is worth what he or she charges. Let's at least talk to him or her before we decide." And that's all we want as salespeople, isn't it? A chance to present. That's when you know the marketing is working. The phone rings, and you are given the opportunity to present.

In the marketing section, we will go into more detail about how to create a marketing campaign that will accomplish that. In the sales section, we will go into detail about how to close the sale once you are there. The point here is that setting up a Web site is something that can and should be done prior to getting into the business.

C. It Should Have an Autoresponder

What is an autoresponder? It is exactly as it sounds. It is an automatic response program that sends messages automatically to prospects who have gone to your Web site and "engaged," or requested information. You sit and type in the messages. Then, you run an ad. When the prospects see the ad and go to your site and ask for the information you have there, they have engaged. They have given you permission to market to them, not sell to them. Market to them. This software program will begin to send practical, informative, educational articles, reports, and messages to the prospects, educating them about the real estate process, financing, title issues, and the like, while at the same time positioning you as the knowledgeable "expert."

The messages all look custom written from you, just to and for them. However, they were all written ahead of time and loaded into your autoresponder, just waiting for someone to go to your site who needs your help. The autoresponder is a highly leveraged way to get and keep in touch with prospects until they become customers, and afterward, until they become referring clients and raving fanatics.

D. Automated Home-Search Capability

There are several programs that do home searches. Simply put, you have a button on your site called "Automated Home-Search," and when prospective homebuyers click on this, it allows them to enter their criteria. You are then notified and asked to approve or disapprove of the search. When you click to okay the search, your computer searches the

MLS database for listings that match the criteria the buyer entered and e-mails the listings directly to him or her daily. The listings are complete with pictures and directions, along with a message from you (of course). Buyers are skeptical, and as a rule, they do not want to talk to salespeople. They just want the information. Give it to them, inform them, educate them, assist them, and take the time to distinguish, elevate, and separate yourself from all the other "me, too" agents out there, and your business will skyrocket. The automated home search and the autoresponder give the buyer what he or she wants, and they give you the leverage you need. Do the research on this prior to obtaining your license. Then, once licensed, you can be up and running with this search capability.

E. Easy to Find

I had a conversation with the "artists" who posed as Web site developers we hired to create our sites for us. They were expensive and cute and had all the graphics you ever wanted in a Web site. Unfortunately, bandwidth was so narrow back then (1997–1998) that it took forever to download.

That was if you were lucky enough to find it in the first place. The conversation went something like this. "Look, number one, I want to be found. We can make it pretty later. Just get it to where my customers and prospects can find me easily. Patient they are not." When it was finished, it was cute, but it could not be found. Pay if you have to, but get your Web site listed with all the top search engines and again, pay if you have to, but make sure it comes up in the top five or at least top ten. People just won't browse much past that. Most will not go to page two. If you are not on page one, you are not on the Net.

Do these five things and you will have a Web site that becomes a lead-generating machine, which will become a constant, ongoing source of leads instead of just a monthly expense.

6. Learn Mortgage Financing

There are over one hundred ways to finance a home. It isn't necessary to learn them all. Again, think CEO. Who can you put on your team who can advise you and your clients on financing options? Who are the experts? However, it is important to understand how money moves through our financial markets in order to have constructive, intelligent conversations with buyers and sellers.

When it comes to mortgage financing, there are "hard money" lenders and "soft money" lenders. Hard money lenders loan on the property itself. They don't care about you, your credit score, how much debt you have, or how you pay your bills. They loan on the property, usually 70 percent or less, at above-market rates, usually 5 to 10 percent higher than other lenders, and only for a short time, usually one year. These are good loans when buying investment property or when you have to move quickly and avoid the lengthy loan qualification process. The appraisal is done. The lender loans 70 percent for one year, and it's done. Before the year is up, the borrower refinances from a soft money lender. Soft money lenders are the traditional real estate lenders using traditional guidelines. The loan is secured by the real estate being purchased, and the buyer and the property both need to qualify.

There are loan programs for veterans, called VA loans. There are different programs for FHA loans and even more different loans for conventional loans. VA, or Veterans Administration, loans are restricted to veterans of the armed services. With them, veterans can buy homes up to an amount with only $1.00 down payment. The low down payments and the ease at which borrowers can qualify make these loans beneficial to our veterans, the men and women who have served our country.

The Federal Housing Administration, or FHA, loans are loans that vary in amounts in different parts of the country. What make these loans attractive are the low down payments, as little as 3 percent, and the ease by which buyers can qualify for them. On FHA loans, buyers are required to purchase MIP, or Mortgage Insurance Premiums, to protect the lender in case the borrower defaults. These premiums usually amount to approximately 1.5 percent of the loan amount and are financed as part of the purchase. HUD, the Department of Housing and Urban Development, oversees the FHA program.

Conventional loans are loans that are generally for move-up buyers, providing for flexible down payments and terms as varied as the imagination. You can put 20 percent or more down to keep your monthly payments low, or borrow as much as 106 percent of the value of the property. If your credit score is high, in some cases, the lender will only verify your assets and look at your income tax returns and/or financial statements. These loans, called "stated income" or "No doc" (for No document) or "Low doc" (for Low document), are good for businesspeople who don't show high incomes on their W-2 forms, yet have lots of cash flow from their businesses, real estate, and other investments.

Financing can at first seem convoluted and confusing. However, if you become a student of it, you may find, as I have, that it is truly an amazing and fascinating subject.

To sum it all up, if you are working with a veteran, get a VA loan. If it is a first-time homebuyer, get an FHA loan. If it is a move-up buyer, get a conventional loan.

Can you see why I recommend one of the first things you do is get your team together? You will have many, many questions. I still do, and I have been doing this quite a while. My lender, who is educated, highly skilled, professional, and responsive is a valuable member of my team, just like my CPA and lawyer and title company. I ask my lender lots of questions. One of the things new agents can be doing to prepare is becoming familiar with different types of financing.

7. Learn the Language of Business

Talk to lenders. Study financing. You need to know how mortgages are originated, priced, processed, underwritten, and approved. You need to be able to articulate it to your clients. Watch CNBC, MSNBC, CNNFN, Bloomberg, and other financial and business channels. Watch how the stock market's rise and fall affects global, national, and local economies. Learn how interest rates affect spending and how the federal government controls the economy by raising and lowering interest rates and how money flows through our system of commerce. Our population as a whole, and real estate buyers and sellers in particular, want to do business with agents who are educated, informed businesspeople and know what is happening and can articulate it.

What are you going to say when the sellers, who are contemplating putting their home on the market, ask, "So, what is the market doing? Is this a good time to sell?" Are you going to say yes because you need the listing, or can you explain the picture in business and financial terms that show you have an opinion based on your observations and research?

I have never taken a loan application or qualified a buyer. I didn't need to. Lenders were happy to provide that service for me. Call your lender. He or she will be happy to meet you, meet your client, or do whatever is necessary to get your buyer pre-approved before you begin shopping for housing. Most people are able to do it online. That's right, pre-approved, not pre-qualified. Pre-qualified doesn't mean a thing. I have a great relationship with my lender. I give the buyer the lender's name and number, and I give the lender the buyer's name and number, and they talk. When the lender has the buyer approved and has extolled the virtues of working with me, the buyer calls me and tells me how much money he or she has qualified for and how much he or she wants to put down. Based on the two, we arrive at a price range. Now, before we ever leave the parking lot, the buyer is approved, he or she has funds, we've agreed on a price range, and we've agreed to a date by which a decision will be made. Your lender is a very valuable member of your team.

8. Learn the Closing Process

The next member of your team is the title company representative, escrow officer, or real estate attorney. Generally speaking, the closing processes are very similar from state to state. In some states, real estate agents write contracts and follow them through to closing. In other states, they simply write one-page binders, and an attorney writes the contract and closes the transaction. Either way, the buyer and seller agree on price, dates, and terms, sometimes subject to the buyer obtaining a mortgage, and almost always subject to the buyers' approval of a property inspection.

After the inspection is approved by the buyer, information is gathered from a variety of sources and prepared for the closing date specified in the contract. Therefore, whether it is a real estate attorney or a title company that is handling the closing, the process is pretty much the same no matter where you live or where you go in the country.

The purpose of the title company is to gather information from the agents, who represent the buyers and sellers, and the mortgage lender and prepare the closing of escrow. The title agent gets this information from the contract, which spells out in detail which party pays for what specific closing expenses. There will be loan costs, which normally are costs incurred and paid for by the borrower.

Sometimes the buyer will ask the seller to assist him or her in obtaining financing, and, if so, the contract will state which costs and the amount the sellers have agreed to pay. There will be title company costs, split between both parties per the contract, and there will be tax and insurance prorations, all figured, collected, and paid by the title company's escrow officer or attorney from each party's proceeds at closing. Specific procedures and processes vary from state to state. It is suffice to say that understanding the buyer's side and the seller's side of the transaction, the documents associated with each, and what they are used for will enable you to solve various problems should or when they occur. Being involved, informed, educated, and proactive will keep your customers calm, your closings on time, and your referrals intact.

The title company can also be a tremendous help to you in your business. I have more of a partnership relationship with my title company than a customer/vendor one. Interview at least three. Ask what kind of support services they have for agents. Tell them that if they help you get your business started up and running, you will be loyal to them and, in return, will recommend your sellers close with them. The process is different across the country, but this is how it works in Austin, Texas. The agent is the customer, not the seller.

Agents are in a position to refer lots of business to title companies, so title companies take good care of their customers, the agents, as well as the sellers and buyers. As a listing agent, I always referred and recommended my preferred title company.

I went to the title company when I started in the business and asked for help. I told them that if they would take care of me, I would take care of them. They took very good care of me. My title company was very instrumental in helping me build my business. They printed my direct mail cards, property-amenities flyers, property-profile books that contained deed restrictions, and the deed and the homeowner's association documents, and ordered virtual video tours, provided mailing labels, and most importantly, provided turnover statistics for any given neighborhood. They answered any and all questions regarding closing costs to both buyer and seller, provided solutions to title and survey problems, held open houses, and sponsored educational events like seminars for buyers and sellers.

Although we needed each other, over the years of working together, handling crises, solving problems, and helping make people's dreams come true, we developed a friendship and a deep level of respect for each other. I will always be grateful to them for their support. Recent changes in the law have affected how and what title companies can do to assist agents in marketing and promoting themselves, and laws may vary from state to state, so be sure to check and see what services they can provide.

To Recap:

Eight things that can be done to prepare prior to obtaining the license:

One. Assemble your team. Use people you already know or ask for referrals.

Two. Preview property.

Three. Learn the contracts.

Four. Learn the city.

Five. Set up your Web site and see that it meets these five criteria:

1. Editable

2. Content rich

3. Equipped with an autoresponder

4. Automated home-search capability

5. Easy to find

Six. Learn the basics of mortgage financing.

Seven. Learn the language of business.

Eight. Learn the basics of the closing process.

TESTIMONIALS

"Frequently, a teacher can steer a person into a new direction, and I feel that Wayne Morgan did just that for me. I think that this one course has profoundly changed my life both in my personal and business relationships. Wayne has an intensive ability to unlock freedom of attitude that enhanced my potential in sales beliefs and attitudes. After attending his course, I closed 45 sales, or 2½ million dollars. I have attended courses in Salado, Dallas, Arlington, and Austin. The Austin Institute of Real Estate is the best. I have attended several courses from this school, and **all** have been very good. I have learned from the experienced teachers how to become successful and give myself personal satisfaction. I am not interested in just earning a living—I want more!!! This one course revived my dreams to make vital life changes, and I rediscovered my purpose in life. I strongly suggest that if you want to enhance your personal relationships or if you have lost your enthusiasm in your business attitude … take this course."

Jacque Weinstrom, Realtor

Coldwell Banker Hallmark Realty

✹ ✹ ✹ ✹ ✹ ✹ ✹ ✹ ✹ ✹ ✹ ✹ ✹ ✹ ✹ ✹ ✹ ✹ ✹ ✹

"This is the best investment in education that any Realtor® could ever make. Don't attend for the hours of credit—attend for the education and your success!"

Kay Kerr

★★★★★★★★★★★★★★★★★★★★★★★

"I found the answer I was looking for. I highly recommend this to all."
Kathryn Bender

★★★★★★★★★★★★★★★★★★★★★★

"The best course/seminar I have ever attended."
Herb Adey

★★★★★★★★★★★★★★★★★★★★★★★

"This course will change my life. I got way more than I expected to ever receive from any one class."
Melinda Walter

Chapter Six

Experience: The Best Teacher

Employees transitioning from the employee environment (where they have been trained) to the business environment (where they are untrained) are often specialists who performed quite well at their former jobs. However, they are unprepared for the business world. Being a good employee often requires specialization, whereas businesses require generalization. If you are employed by a company, and there are other employees performing all the different functions of the company, all you have to worry about and focus on is doing your job well. You specialize in one area. However, once you enter the business world and begin building your business, you must perform **all** the functions of the business. You can no longer be a specialist. You must become a generalist.

You have to know and understand marketing, sales, customer service, bookkeeping, accounting, tax strategies, law (there will be legal documents), negotiations, and systems creation and management. You have to know all the different aspects of the company and how they fit together to form the whole. Instead of one employee among many performing one of many tasks, you are one person by yourself performing all the tasks.

The biggest problem most **new** agents have is in the lead-generation area. As employees, they were good administrators, but in this sales-driven business, you have to get the phone to ring. Most agents cannot get the phone to ring. Many are disappointed when they complete their licensing requirements, pass their exam, get their business cards, and get ready …

and the phone doesn't automatically start ringing off the hook with buyers and sellers clamoring to do business with them.

There is a lot of information to learn in a short amount of time. If you have a background in marketing and sales, if you can generate leads and close them, if you can generate income, and if you can put a team together, you can survive until you can get your business up and running. However, if you have no experience, the phone doesn't ring, and there are no sales, it will be tough going. Because the learning curve is so long, most people run out of money before they run out of time. The length of time between obtaining the license and closing the first transaction and getting the first check is so great, most can't go that long without income. Education and experience make the time between licensure and getting paid shorter. That's why experience is so crucial. There is so much to learn.

The Solution

There are two things a new agent with no experience can do to learn the business: learn fast or get a position as an assistant to a top producer who will teach you the ropes. You can work to earn, or you can work to learn. Money won't make you rich. Knowing how to make money will. In Austin alone, there are approximately 4,500 licensed agents and brokers. Home sales average 1,200 per month. You do the math, and we aren't even talking about the multi-million-dollar producers yet. The competition is intense, and you have to have the skills to compete.

Become an Apprentice

Either bring the skills with you, get them before you enter the game, or learn them at a high rate of speed. An apprenticeship program is an ancient and proven method of acquiring skills. I have had some positions where I paid to work because I wanted to learn.

Be grateful if an experienced agent will even hire you. Why should they? You don't know anything. Become a student of the business. Ask them what you can do to help them grow the business. Come from total service, become a lifelong learner, and volunteer to do anything and everything to bring in new business or make the existing customers ecstatic. Your job description is this: If you see something that needs to be done, it's your job.

Go to every seminar, read every book and listen to every CD you find on the subject of real estate. Look for problems to solve and solve them. Make yourself valuable. If you are an employee and you want to avoid being downsized, focus on making yourself more valuable to the company. Even amidst massive cutbacks, if you are valuable to the organization, they will find some place to put you. If you are the business owner, focus on making yourself more valuable. We focus on making sure our customers make more money. Our job is not to take money from our customers but to also help them make money. The same goes with our vendors. We want to make them money. Our vendors and our customers consider us to be valuable.

TESTIMONIALS

"This course is life changing. I wish I'd had this info 30 years ago, but my kids will—I'll make sure they do."
Linda Sykes

"Best real estate/non-real estate course I have ever experienced. It came to me at the right time in my life in my quest for financial freedom."
Tom Amiss
#1 Agent Austin Citywide

"I wish I had been exposed to this 15 years ago. Wayne's principles should be required reading in our public schools."
Steve Rennells

"Very remarkable and stimulating class."
R. Romero

"I wanted to take a moment to express my gratitude. Your psychology of investing course has given me a new lease on life. I have always been able to generate income, but until now, I have not known how to 'spend my money.' Thanks to your course, in the near future, I will no longer need to work for money, as my money will be working for me. You and Lynn have done an exceptional job in creating a course that not only handles the nuts and bolts of investing, but also as the course title states, changes your inner psychology as well. I appreciated the fact that you shared your own personal experiences regarding past failures and present successes. I know I speak for others when I say this allowed a certain comfort level, which allowed 'guards to be dropped' and information to be absorbed. With your use of humor and emotion, you were masterful in linking all the information together. In closing, 'WOW! WHAT A COURSE!' Again, thank you for creating 'Psychology of Investing.'"

Dean Erickson

Director of Property Management

Henry S. Miller, Realtors

Chapter Seven

Marketing: The Number One Skill to Have

Marketing and sales are the two biggest challenges facing real estate agents. Most do not know how to get the phone to ring and get face-to-face with a buyer or seller. And often, when they do, they can't close the sale. At the end of the day, a sale is a sale, and if you are going to be in sales, you need to know how to lead people to make the right decision. I consider these two areas the most important because they are income generators. Even if the inside of your business is a totally confusing, discombobulated mess with no organization and no system and is in complete chaos, if you can market and sell, you are making money. Every business has its share of problems, but most don't have any that lots of money can't solve. Not being able to generate a constant stream of leads and convert them into sales that add income to the company coffers will drive most from the business in frustration.

"How do I get the phone to ring?" Annette asked. "I've run ads on my listings, I am in the local homes magazine, I have a Web site, and I am spending lots of money on direct mail, but it doesn't seem to be working."

"Me, too," said Blake. "I am paying a marketing company thousands each month to generate leads for me, and that's not working, either."

"What business are you in?" I asked the class. Each student had a different answer.

"The service business."

"The real estate business."

"The referral business."

"The dreams business."

"The finance business."

I waited until they stopped.

"You are in the same business I'm in. You are in the lead-generation and education business," I told them.

"Marketing is an area where almost every company flounders. Open any Yellow Pages directory and read the ads. Often, they all sound the same, look the same, read the same, and make the same promises. 'We're number one,' 'We have the most,' 'We sell the most,' 'We're the biggest,' 'No one has more,' 'We do it all,' 'Best service,' 'Best quality and price-guaranteed!' 'We do it right,' 'Honest and dependable,' 'Convenient location,' 'Easy to find,' and on and on. First of all, these ads are not believed by consumers. Second, the consumer can't distinguish between them because they all look alike, sound alike, and do the same thing. These adjectives that companies use may be important to the company or the ad or marketing department, but they do nothing to answer the consumer's number one question: 'What's in it for me?' Consumers hear so many of these generalities that after a while they tend to not believe any of them. Therefore, when you use them, you create doubt and disbelief.

Claude Hopkins, one of the best marketers/advertisers of the twentieth century, said, 'Platitudes and generalities roll off the human understanding like water off of a duck's back. They make no impression whatsoever.'

Until you can and do answer the 'WIIFM' (What's in it for me?) question, you and your company will continue to be seen as the same as your competition (not similar-same).

I was buying ceiling fans for some investment properties I was remodeling. There were 110 models suspended from the ceiling at the hardware store. 110! How in the world was I going to decide which one to buy? Other than a few strange designs, they all looked alike. Since I could not distinguish one from the other and they were going into rental houses, I did what most people who can't tell the difference do: I defaulted to price. I bought the cheapest ones.

I dropped my phone in the pool and went to the local nationwide electronics chain for a replacement. Same problem. Fifty-five cordless models. There were another fifty or so cord models. Since they all seemed the same to me, except for the number of buttons (which only confused me more), I asked the same question: 'Since they are all about the same, all the warranties are the same, they all do the same thing, WHICH ONE IS THE CHEAPEST?'

I went to a superstore to buy some sneakers. There were five aisles full of sport-type shoes. Running shoes, walking shoes, jogging shoes, tennis shoes, basketball shoes, soccer shoes, cross-trainer shoes, and on and on they went. All the name brands, every size, shape, and color imaginable. I didn't know the difference, and there was not a salesman in sight. Guess what I did? Found a pair that fit. Were they the cheapest? No. However, price was a consideration. Why pay more just for a particular logo? It makes no difference to me who makes the shoe.

I just want one that fits well, lasts a reasonable amount of time, and cleans up easily. After that, to me they are all the same. So, once again, it boils down to price. There is nothing done to make them different. They all look like 'me, too' products."

In the Beginning ...

When I was growing up, there were four channels on television: 2, 11, 13, and a public service channel.

It was easy to memorize what was on. We were transitioning from a nation that made things to a nation that bought things. Labor-saving devices were introduced, and the push was on to save time by working less and having more free time. It didn't happen, of course, but that was the message.

People started buying soap, bread, clothes, and a host of other things instead of making them. If you had any new product that was at all decent and advertised it enough, it became a huge success.

It was called "interruption marketing," and the marketers made no bones about it. "We interrupt this program to bring you an important commercial message." Remember those? They didn't even apologize!

I never once heard anyone say, "Sorry to interrupt, but there is this new gadget we have that will ..." They just told us they were going to interrupt, and then they did it. Most haven't stopped because, for a long time, this method worked.

Interruption marketing used to work, but it doesn't work anymore. The less it works, the more money the marketers throw at it, and the more money they throw at it, the less it works.

Here are some estimates. There were over 17,000 new grocery products introduced last year, and over $1,000 to promote them was directed exclusively at you. The average consumer sees about 1 million marketing messages per year, or about 3,000 a day. An hour of television may contain forty or more, while the local paper, over one hundred. Add to that a few telemarketing calls, the ads at the grocery store, billboards, radio, junk mail, and buses and cars, and it doesn't take long to add up. And it all adds up to whole lot of noise. The noise gets louder as more and more competitors compete for finite dollars. It's a zero-sum game. When a box of Rice Krispies sells, a box of Grape Nuts doesn't. It becomes a game of winners and losers, all competing for the consumer's attention and interrupting at every step, clamoring at us to stop what we are doing and listen. Where we used to listen politely to telemarketers before telling them we were not interested, we now just hang up or get on the "no call" list. When a commercial comes on, we surf.

The ads in the paper hardly ever even get read. If we don't know who is sending that piece of mail, it gets tossed or left unopened. When commercials hit the radio, we move to another channel or don't listen. We don't hear, and ten seconds after the commercial ends, we couldn't remember what was said. We have 260 plus television stations, most of which we don't watch, and we even throw out magazines we ordered, still unread. We are totally and completely in the Information Age, and we are overwhelmed by it.

We say we need more time, but in most cases what we really need is more space in our brains. The hard drive is full. It is almost impossible to take on any more data. Unfortunately, the effort to get us to do just that is there, and it is unrelenting. Marketers are hoping the success of the past will translate into success in the future.

As consumers, we have done well. It really doesn't matter much where we buy what we buy. It's all pretty good quality, the prices are all about the same, and, for the most part, it's going to function and last a good while.

It's the marketing that isn't working. Spending millions, or even billions, to get eyeballs that don't buy doesn't work. The "dot coms" found this out the hard way. Consumers are unable to distinguish one product or service from another. Even when they do want or need to buy, all the ads are alike.

So, they shop price because the marketing piece did not clearly define the benefit to the buyer and/or give the consumer a compelling reason to call. Price becomes the differentiator.

The Solution

As a business or as a real estate agent, rather than try to be all things to all people and sell more things to more people, you're better off targeting your market. In trying to be all things to everyone, you end up being nothing to everybody. It is better to be focused, specific, and unique. What specific problems do you or your company solve? What value do you bring to the transaction, and how do you articulate that in a way that makes people want to call you?

How do you do that?

Shift from interruption marketing to permission marketing. Stop doing what the other marketers are doing. Stop interrupting people. Find out what they need. Help them. Educate them. People want to sell houses. People want to buy houses. You don't have to sell them on the fact that they need a house. You just have to find people who want to either buy or sell a house. It's a process that, if done well, will elevate, separate, and differentiate you from every other agent out there and drive an endless stream of customers to your door.

Lifetime Value

What is the lifetime value of a customer? How much does the average pizza eater spend on pizzas over the course of his or her life? Approximately $1,200. When the phone rings at the local pizza parlor, it is not a $20.00 order; it's a $1,200 order!

What does the average Cadillac owner spend on Cadillacs over the course of his or her life? Approximately $330,000! It's not a $30,000 order; it's a $330,000 order. The first thing to do is determine the lifetime value of your customer. One of the biggest assets in any company is its existing customers, yet many companies spend incredible amounts of money attracting new customers when they could very easily sell more to the ones they already have. This concept makes sense, but how do you apply it to real estate, where people only move every five to seven years?

Determine the Lifetime Value

What is the value of a customer who will refer just two people to you? Let's say, for example, you are in the $150,000 price range, and you receive a 3 percent selling commission, and you are on a 70/30 split with your broker. For every transaction that closes at that price, you will net $3,150. If that person referred you two people that bought or sold in the same price range, that would make you $6,300.

If they sent you two people who sent two and so on and so on, pretty soon you would have more people referring people to you than you could handle. If you are thinking to yourself, "That's just like multi-level marketing," then you are right. Multi-level marketing, or MLM, is also called "network marketing" precisely for that reason.

What would you rather do? You could cold call, prospecting for new business by trying to convince someone you do not know why he or she should either buy or sell a home and use you to represent him or her in the process, or receive an introduction and a heartfelt recommendation from someone who has worked with you, is pleased, and will refer you to someone who has already made the decision to move?

You can do one of two things: continue to prospect by cold calling people who don't know you or focus on delivering world-class service and building a referral base from people who know you. The referral is the lifeblood of your business.

How Do You Sell More Homes to People Who Already Have One?

One, educate them about the advantages of investing in real estate for their retirement. It doesn't take much. One house per year for ten years will outperform most other investments. If they started at age forty, bought one per year until they were fifty, and put them all on fifteen-year mortgages, they would all be paid off at age sixty-five, just in time for retirement. If they each rented on average of $800 per month, that should bring in about $5,500 per month in net passive income.

Focus on Making <u>Them</u> Wealthy

How often do people move, on average? Five to seven years. You can sell one house to the same person and wait another five to seven years for him or her to move, or you could get him or her to buy more houses. What if you could invert that ratio? What if you took the time to educate him or her about the benefits of owning real estate, and he or she became an investor? What if, instead of buying one house every five years, he or she bought five per year? Or maybe just four? Or two? Focus on making other people rich, and you will see how you will both prosper.

Educate Them

It is truly one of the easiest ways to retire comfortably. Instead of the traditional closing gifts of door knockers or wine-and-cheese baskets, why not provide them with education? Try giving them a copy of *Rich Dad, Poor Dad* and *Cashflow Quadrant* and the board game Cash Flow 101 by Robert Kiyosaki, and when they become more educated about real estate investments, help them find and invest in real estate. Talk about repeat customers!

Instead of driving buyers around looking at houses, simply fax your investors the hottest new listings of investment properties, complete with an analysis that shows their cash-on-cash returns, their monthly cash flow, their internal rate of return, and the cap rate. After you put them in a few properties that do well, they will be calling you asking you if you have any more deals for them. Instead of you calling people trying to get them to buy, people will be calling you, asking you if you have anything they can buy.

The other way is to develop the customer into a referral machine. If done right, each customer could be developed, taught, and trained to send you business with a heartfelt endorsement of you and your services.

If one totally impressed customer sent you two people who sent you two and so on, how long would it take to build your business into a referral-based business? Can you see why, with all the noise and clutter in the advertising world, your odds are much better off developing a relationship and building confidence in your abilities with people who could refer people to you rather than chase people who don't want to be chased?

The Five Stages of a Customer:

(See Glossary for definitions)

The Five Stages of a Customer

1. Suspect
2. Prospect
3. Customer
4. Client
5. Referring Client

The Process

Most agents are taught to prospect when they get into the real estate business. Cold call, knock on doors, call the For Sale by Owner (also known as the FSBO or fizzbo), call around just listed properties, and call around just sold properties. The problem with that is most of it is interruption marketing, which, we established earlier, is obsolete. The other problem is that it is painful for the agent.

An experienced agent might pull it off because he or she has lots of transaction experience, and he or she knows how to talk with people about the ins and outs of real estate. It makes no sense to turn a rookie without any transaction experience loose on the hardest market of all to crack. They don't know anything about the business. Most FSBOs are FSBOs because they don't have confidence in real estate agents. To send a brand-new agent over there to talk to them about marketing their home just reinforces the FSBO's decision to do it themselves.

Think about it. A brand new agent gives the FSBO a presentation, can't answer any of the FSBO's questions, has no marketing plan, and can't address concerns about repairs to be done, decorating, rearranging furniture, whether or not to paint and carpet, or setting appointments for the showings. Both the agent and the FSBO are confused and frustrated. The end result: The FSBO is probably not going to let the new agent practice on his or her home.

Agents Don't Like Chasing People

Cold calling only works for a small percent of the population. An individual with a High D type personality will cold call because High Ds are motivated by a challenge. I will explain High Ds in the next chapter when I go into sales. For the other three personality types, cold calling is a painful experience. A human being simply will not continue a painful process for an extended period of time. Most people don't like chasing people, and you don't have to.

People Don't Like Being Chased

Furthermore, people don't like being chased. There is a much more sophisticated, elegant way to get the agent some wins early on in the business, build his or her confidence, and establish some momentum. If the goal is to convert them into referring clients, it will take time. Permission marketing is just the opposite of interruption marketing. People just don't have enough time to pay attention to all the messages. However, they do want information.

That's why most ads don't work. The consumer doesn't have time to try to figure out what it is you do, or can do, for him or her. Instead of interrupting the prospect, hoping to grab a moment to shout your message before he or she turns to the next interruption or interrupter, the permission marketer solves the problem the interruption marketer creates. You give the prospects time to pay attention. Find out what it is they want to know. Allow them to educate themselves on their schedule. This is how to start.

Go Where the Pain Is ...

Find out what causes the suspects pain, what they want to know, and what they want to do, and tell them everything they could ever possibly want to know about it—free of charge and obligation. Go where the pain is. Ask the customers what they want.

The more pain, the more payoff. Instead of thinking you already know what your customers want, ask them. Conduct a survey.

How Do You Find the Pain?

Why is it that most real estate marketing newsletters fail to attract leads? The agent wrote it! The agent isn't supposed to write the newsletter. The reader is. How do you know what the reader wants to read? Do a survey. Familiarize yourself with their concerns.

Sample Survey

List everyone you know. Call all of them and ask them a few questions. Here they are:

1. Do you currently receive a real estate newsletter?

     Yes   No

2. If so, do you read it?

     Yes   No

3. What would it need to have in it for you to read it?

_____

_____

_____

4. Do you want to be kept abreast of real estate news that may affect your property?

Yes   No

5. Would it be helpful if it contained the following:

a.   Information about homes that have sold in your area?

Yes   No

b.   Information about financial markets and mortgage rates?

Yes   No

c.   Market trends citywide?

Yes   No

d.   News about your area/subdivision?

Yes   No

e.   Real estate investment tips?

Yes   No

f.   Tax reduction strategies?

Yes   No

6. May I have your permission to send you a newsletter?

     Yes   No

     E-mail OR Snail mail

7. May I call you afterward just for some quick feedback?

     Yes   No

8. When you bought your home, were you represented by a real estate agent?

     Yes   No

9. Would you use that same agent again?

     Yes   No

     Why / why not?

_____

_____

10. Would you use an agent to sell your home?

     Yes   No

     Why / why not?

_____

_____

Now, what is happening? Your future customers are telling you exactly how to market to them! The answers to these questions will tell you what to put into your newsletter. You now have their permission to market them, and you know what they want to know.

The Six Keys to Permission Marketing

1. Make it personal.

2. Make it relevant.

3. Make it anticipated.

4. Have something good to say.

5. Say it well.

6. Say it often.

In chapter five, I wrote about the five steps to building a Web site. The Web site can also act as a newsletter; only it will serve many more people in a cheaper, more efficient way. In your newsletter, refer to the Web site. On the Web site, refer to the newsletter.

You can run simple ads that will tell people how to get more information simply by visiting your Web site. When they engage, they have given you permission to begin marketing to them. Use the six-step process described above to develop the relationship, remove doubt, and lay the foundation for trust.

If You Build It ...

Remember the movie *Field of Dreams* with Kevin Costner? "If you build it, they will come." Build it. Tell them where it is, and they will come. If it is content rich, they will come back. When they come back, they engage. When they engage, they have given you permission to market to them. Give them as much information as you can. People will go where they are fed. Feed them. Instead of trying to trick them into listening to you for just a moment or two, you now have their ear (or eyes) and can calmly tell them what they want to know as well as what you want them to know. This is what makes you different and why they should do business with you, only you, and why they should refer everyone they know to you.

Use the Law of Attraction

By using the law of attraction, you become attractive and therefore gain more mass. The more mass you have, the more attractive you become to others. The more attractive you become, the more mass you gather, and so on. Instead of chasing potential clients in the hopes that they choose you, they become attracted to you because you are not chasing them, and you are providing them with something of value and asking nothing in return. They then perceive you as the expert, and they chase you instead, and you then choose them.

You choose the nicest, most professional, well-educated customers who see you as the expert, call you when they are considering a move and who will follow your advice. If you are thinking they won't call you because you have already told them everything they need to know about buying or selling their home, you may be in for a surprise and here is why …

How to Lose a Client Who Wants to Do Business

My wife, Lynn, and I live on the north shore of Lake Travis just outside Austin, Texas. Lake Travis is one of the cleanest, clearest lakes in Texas with a limestone bottom and clear, blue water. We live high on a hill overlooking the lake and the surrounding hill country with the most stunning views imaginable. Unfortunately, our yacht is in a marina on the south shore, a good one-hour drive away. When we go to the lake, which is quite often, it becomes a two-hour drive, which is a bit much. Especially when you consider that we are just across the lake from our yacht, and it is only a thirteen-minute trip by boat.

After buying and remodeling our home and living on the north shore of the lake and making that trip for two years, I had finally had enough. "I'm buying a boat to get to the boat," I announced one day. "I can't take driving all the way around the lake anymore."

As fate would have it, the very next day, a catalog from the local marine supply retailer appeared in the mailbox. Inside were pictures of rubber dinghies and motors, just exactly what I was looking for! I was so excited as I drove down to the store to pick out my new boat and motor. I was even more excited thinking that I was about to rid myself of some frustration. I love going to and spending time out on the lake on the yacht. We load up the food, drive around the lake, stow it all away, wash it down, check all the systems, remove all the covers, and cruise to our favorite secluded little cove where we tie up and stay for days, enjoying the water, the sun, and each other. Then we return to civilization and reverse the whole process, including that horrible drive back around the lake. It's not so bad if we are going away for a few days, but it makes an evening cruise almost impossible because of the time it takes getting back and forth.

So, when I saw the catalog and my problem was about to be solved, I was happy! My transportation troubles were almost over. Thank you, marine supply store, for sending me that catalog!

With those thoughts in mind and a picture of me motoring at high speed across the lake in my new boat loaded with ice chests and my wife at the bow, I drove into town to the store. I pointed to the rubber inflatable dinghy pictured there and asked, "Is this a flat-bottom boat?" Yes, they assured me it was.

"Will it fit in the back of my SUV when it is inflated?" Yes, they assured me it would. "Can I put a ten-horsepower engine on it?" Yes, no problem, it is rated for a ten-horsepower engine. "Great!" Now, I was really excited. I explained my idea. "I just need something to get me, my wife, and a couple ice chests back and forth across the lake. Will this boat be good for that?" I was so hoping the answer was yes.

"Yes. That is what they are made for."

I was coming out of my skin.

"How much?"

They told me how much. It was way more than I thought I could get it for.

My enthusiasm dampened, but not enough to deter me. If I could make the purchase quickly, maybe I could get out of there before buyer remorse set in and I ended up talking myself out of it like I tended to do with major purchases.

"I'll take it," I said a little less enthusiastically.

"We have to order it. We don't have any in stock."

"How long?" I asked, even less enthusiastically.

It was Wednesday. I was hoping to go from the store straight to the lake, which was practically deserted on weekdays.

"We can have it in two days."

I considered this. Friday. I could go to the lake early, beat the crowd, and try out my new boat. "Okay. I guess I'll take it."

They called the warehouse in a distant city. No boat. They were out of stock. The salesman put me on the phone with the person from the warehouse.

"I've got one left that's last year's model I can make you a good deal on," he told me. He gave me the discount. I took it.

Friday, the store called. The boat had arrived. I went to the store to pick it up. I was excited. The vision was back. I saw myself once again flying across the lake. I had my boat! I got a good deal on it! We loaded the boat into the SUV.

"Where's the motor?" I asked, chomping at the bit to get out of there.

They all looked at me in silence. "Motor? You want a motor? What size?"

I thought to myself, "Wow. Talk about a short attention span." And I said, "Ten horse. Just like we talked about."

They looked at each other again, then back at me.

"We don't carry anything that big. We'll have to order it."

My weekend trip across the lake in the new boat vanished. I then pictured myself driving there and back, two hours stuck in traffic in the car. Eventually, the motor came in, and I picked it up and took it home. I was so ready for the lake. I unpacked the boat, and what was sold to me as "last year's model" was actually a used boat.

I blew up the boat, and it wouldn't fit into the SUV. Too big. I deflated the boat. I took the boat, the pump, and the motor to the lake. I inflated the boat again. I put the motor on the boat. I put the paddles and my wife into the boat. The boat had a V-shaped bottom. Only instead of the V being on the outside of the boat, the V was on the inside of the boat, creating a hump running straight through the boat from bow to stern, just like the cars used to do before they changed the way they made them. The motor was too large for the little boat, and every time I gave it throttle, it did a wheelie.

After the initial start, however, it would not push the boat through the water because the prop spun so fast, it actually pushed water away from the boat instead of pushing the boat through the water. With a little less excitement, I returned to the dock, packed everything in the SUV, and went home.

The next day, I went back to the store and explained what had happened. "No problem!" I was told. "We'll just give you a smaller engine and credit you for the difference."

That engine was too small and had the same problem as the first engine: It just spun and wouldn't push the boat. Also, the fact that it was a used boat with a hump running down the middle made it undesirable. I took the whole thing back to the store.

"No problem," I was told after I described the ongoing problem with the engine. "You should have put a 'whale tail' on the engine. That happens all the time."

The excitement was gone. It had been replaced with frustration, confusion, and a little anger.

"Look, this is not what I told you I wanted. I told you I wanted a flat-bottom boat big enough to carry me, my wife, and a couple of ice chests across the lake that would fit into the back of my SUV. This won't do any of that. Either make it do it or give me a refund."

The salesman got on the phone with the boss from the distant city. There was much loud talking, a raising of voices, and a few expletives between the two parties. They came back to me standing at the counter. "Sorry, bud," he said to me. "My boss says you bought the boat. There is nothing I can do."

The excitement was gone. I left the store, concerned I might say or do something that would be irreversible and that I might have regretted. They mailed me the catalog. They got me to come to the store. They did not listen to me. They did not discover my wants and needs. They did not educate me. They blamed me when they failed to deliver.

We eventually got it all worked out. I kept the ten-horsepower engine, but bought the flat-bottom boat and all the coast-guard-required accessories somewhere else. I have owned my yacht for three years. I spent an average of $2,500 per year at that store. I am not saying I will never frequent that store again, but I will only buy what I absolutely have to have that I cannot find anywhere else. My lifetime value to them has diminished to the point of being almost nonexistent.

Under-Promise, Over-Deliver

Does this story sound familiar? We really don't have to look too far to learn how to become rich in business and investing. There are plenty of reverse role models out there. They didn't take time to educate me. What information they did provide was inaccurate. I wanted them to solve my problem. I was willing to pay. They made it worse, then they blamed me.

The lesson here is another valuable key to marketing. Most companies and salespeople over-promise and under-deliver. This is one reason people do not like salespeople. They will say or do almost anything to get the business, then they treat the customer badly. You may have run into someone like this yourself. Companies and individuals that over-promise and under-deliver typically do not have a steady stream of referrals coming their way.

It is why their customers do not become clients for life and why they always have to hustle deals. If you want to become a master marketer, then remember it is key to under-promise and over-deliver. Continue to exceed their expectations by educating them and providing world-class service instead of letting them down or making it difficult for them to do business with you, and you will have raving, fanatical referring clients for life.

The key to marketing is that there isn't one tool that can be used to generate a steady, ongoing stream of calls. A marketing campaign, plan, or system, as we call it, has many components. It isn't any one piece, strategy, or technique that makes or breaks a good marketing campaign. It is a series of strategies all working in conjunction with each other, complementing each other, and adding a part to the whole.

The school my wife, Lynn, and I own (The Austin Institute of Real Estate) has averaged 70 percent market share over the past three years. That is a statistic most companies would be proud of. And we are, but what I am more pleased with is the amount of wallet share we have. For us, it's not just about getting a customer. It's more about getting the customer BACK. Our surveys show that once we get them to our classroom, we get them for the duration of their licensing process and their continuing education thereafter. They become lifelong, fanatical referring clients.

The Purpose of the Business

The inside of the company has to perform at peak efficiency, constantly exceeding the consumer's expectations in a big way. It is absolutely imperative that you become so passionate about the quality of service that you provide that you would work all day and night without rest, food, or water in order to ensure that each and every customer who enters your sanctuary comes away thinking, "Wow. That was incredible. I'm telling everyone I know about this place (person)." It becomes the culture, the driving force, the whole reason for even being in business. IT IS NOT ABOUT MAKING MONEY. The true purpose of a business is to serve. Money is a byproduct. All it tells you is how well you are serving and strengthening others.

The Two Sides of a Business

There are two sides to any business. There is the inside systems and the outside perception. The inside is the internal workings, the nuts and bolts of what you do. It is your systems, processes, production, taking and filling orders, marketing, customer service, sales, accounting, etc. The outside perception is how the public perceives you. Not many companies do both the inside and the outside well. They either do the inside well and can't articulate it, or they articulate well (I call it 'creative marketing') and when you get there, they can't or don't do what they say in their ad. They can't seem to process the customer. I see this every now and again.

I see or read a great ad, I get impressed, it wows me, and I go to that business and get totally disappointed. This is the reason I told you the boat story. Businesses have two main problems when it comes to marketing: They either do something very unique and very, very well and can't articulate it to the public, so the public thinks they are just like everyone else; or the ad pulls, the customer shows up, and the inside operations are so poor, they lose the very customer they are paying to come into the store!

In order to succeed in the Information/Permission Age, you must articulate what it is you do well, say what the benefit is to the consumer, and go above and beyond the call of duty when consumers show up. My experiences with businesses as a consumer have been less than gratifying as of late. It seems there are so many consumers consuming that the attitude I get whenever I shop or ask questions to get more information in order to make a better decision is, "Yeah, yeah, yeah, NEXT!" If your marketing pieces are filled with promises, generalities, and platitudes that sound like everyone else's that offer the same product or service, you will not be believed by the public. Their perception of you is that you are the same as everyone else. To overcome being seen as the same as your competitor, you will need to develop a Unique Marketing Position.

Your Unique Marketing Position

How do you articulate what it is you do and the benefit to the customer? Simple. Pretend your product or service is on trial. The jury is the consumer, and you are the attorney defending the product or service. It is a life or death matter. If the jury votes in favor of your product or service, you go free, if not, the electric chair. What compelling argument will you use that will convince this group that they should vote for you? That is your unique marketing position. What you think or know about how well your business is producing is totally irrelevant. The only perception that matters is the consumers' perception, and they perceive you via what you say or do in your ads and marketing materials. Remember, you can't use words like *biggest*, *longest*, *most*, *fastest*, *shortest*, *highest quality*, *great service*, *low prices*, *lowest prices*, and so on without answering the WIIFM question. Why? You are using platitudes and generalities that everyone else is using, and the consumer doesn't believe you. If you can put together a marketing campaign, a system that elevates you, distinguishes you, separates you, and differentiates you from all your competitors, answers their concerns and solves their problems, they will do business with you, **regardless of your commission rate.**

What Is *Your* UMP?

"How do I develop my UMP?" Annette asked.

"Did you complete your surveys?" I asked her.

"Yes. I surveyed twenty people in my sphere of influence. They all said pretty much the same thing."

"Great! What were the three things they all had in common?"

Annette got out her surveys. "The common denominator was they wanted some kind of assurance. Most of them had a bad experience after listing their home with a Realtor® in the past and could not get out of the contract. They felt like they got stuck with someone who made promises but only wanted to get a listing, not provide customer service and get their home sold."

"Perfect! That's what you need to know. Your UMP answers those concerns. If you have twenty people saying the same thing, design your marketing around that. It sounds to me like they are unhappy, maybe even in a little pain. They have a problem. Solve it. That's your UMP. Let's start with the first one. You said they said something about their not being able to get out of the contract. What can you do with that?"

"How about this?" asked Jim. "I won't ask you to sign a contract."

"Good, but can you do that?" I asked him. "Remember, developing the UMP accomplished two things. You find out what the market wants via your research. You also find out whether or not you can deliver it. You better be able to do what you say in your UMP, or you become like the marine supply store I told you about. Under-promise and over-deliver. Most companies over-promise and under-deliver; that's why people don't believe the ads. The second thing developing and using a UMP does is it forces you to look at the inside reality of your business. Can you really deliver what you say in your UMP? You have some exposure here. Can you get paid if you don't have a contract? Can you even legally put a sign in their yard and market their property?"

"Probably not," Jim admitted.

"Don't stop. I like the way you're thinking. Let's keep working on that until we've got it to where we can deliver it. Start with a headline. Everyone work on this. Get together in groups and brainstorm. Come up with UMPs that answer the 'I was unhappy and couldn't get out of my listing contract' problem and the pain that comes with it."

They worked for quite a while, talking, opinionating, and throwing ideas around.

Finally, a hand went up. "Okay, how about this? Tell them that if for any reason they are not happy, they can cancel the agreement at any time."

"Can you do that?" I asked.

"Sure. It puts the onus on me to perform. If I don't, they get to walk away."

"I agree. Great UMP. Now, word it in such a way that you can put it on all your marketing pieces. Remember: People don't buy things; they buy results."

After a short while, they had it. "I won't ask you to sign a contract and disappear behind broken promises. If for any reason you are unhappy with my service, you may cancel this agreement at any time. Guaranteed."

"Excellent!" I said. "Now, why not take it a step further and really separate yourself from the pack. Why not create a nice certificate that you all sign and title it your 'Easy-Exit Listing Guarantee'?"

Find your UMP and be able to articulate it in thirty seconds or less. Your customers have neither the time nor inclination to try to figure out what you do, how you do it, or what the benefit is to them. Additionally, if you say what all the agents are saying, you will seem to be the same as them. What are you going to do or say that will set you apart from the competition? If you do not do that, the public sees you as the same, and so, to them, it doesn't make any difference to them who they choose to represent them.

How do you find your UMP? Listen to your customers. Hear their concerns and considerations. Solve their problem. The solution to *their* problem is *your* UMP. Ask your customers. Do a survey. Make your UMP unique and valuable.

Some Additional Questions to Ask

What are you looking for in an agent?

How will you know when you have it?

What are the five biggest problems you have to deal with when selling/ buying a home?

What do you want to achieve by selling/buying a home?

Have you sold a home recently? What, if any, problems did you encounter?

Have you bought a home recently? What, if any, problems did you encounter?

Develop your UMP. Find something good to say. Then say it well and say it often.

Why You Are Asked to Reduce Your Commission

I have heard some very good comebacks, responses, and answers from many very good sales trainers regarding what to say when the sellers ask you to reduce your commission. I even have a few good ones myself. The problem is, once the question is asked, it is too late. What the seller is saying is, "We don't believe you are worth what you are asking us to pay." Traditional sales trainers teach how to "overcome" this "objection."

Rather than learn to overcome the objection, I believe the question that needs to be asked is, "Why are they asking you to reduce your commission in the first place?"

This is why: You do not have a UMP, and to the sellers, you and all the other agents they interviewed said the same things. All of you sound alike, look alike, and promise the same things. Just like the ceiling fans, the cordless phones, and the sneakers, they all seem to be the same. Since you are all the same in the eyes of the seller, they default to price, just like most of us. So they ask: "Will you reduce your commission?"

Establish a powerful unique marketing position and the value you bring to the transaction, and be able to articulate it well with passion and sincerity, and sellers will not be asking you to cut your price—instead, they will send you referrals like you won't believe!

(*Hint*: At The Austin Institute of Real Estate, 62 percent of our business is from referrals, and we are the most expensive real estate school in town. People don't want a cheap price. Price has little to do with making buying decisions. People want value for their money. Become more valuable to them, and they will pay you more.)

If you are getting asked to reduce your commission, you don't have a UMP. People are getting laid off and suffering financially because they aren't adding value to the organization. Organizations keep their most valuable people, regardless of salary. It's not about the price. It's about the value you bring. Work on becoming more and more valuable to all your clients and customers. Start with a simple message—a UMP.

Direct Response

"Can we use that same process with ads?" Jim asked. "I am spending a fortune on real estate ads, and they are not pulling. I get very few calls. When they do call, all they want is the address. My broker says not to give it to them, but when I don't, they get mad. Then when I do give it to them, they never call back. What should I do?"

First and foremost, stop reading other people's ads because yours will read and sound like theirs. Subscribe to newspapers from cities far away from you. Most of their ads will read and sound the same, but they will be different from yours.

Most ads are what I call institutional ads. They read like this: Sentence sentence sentence, sentence sentence sentence, sentence, sentence. Sentence sentence sentence, sentence sentence sentence, sentence sentence sentence.

Never, never, ever run an ad that does not contain a direct response trigger. What is a direct response ad? It is very simply an ad that gives the reader, viewer, or listener, depending on the media, a reason to contact you. Buyers looking for homes read the ads, but they only call on a few, and the ones they call on the most are written in a certain, specific way. We can go on for days about how to write an ad, but the main thing is this: Always and only write a direct response ad and have something of value to give away when they contact you, or respond. You want a listing or a qualified buyer? Attract them to you incrementally. Run a direct response ad, refer them to your Web site, and give them what they want (which is usually more information). They will then engage (take the information), thereby granting you permission to respond, and you begin the conversation, you begin the relationship. It starts with a reason to call. That's the direct response part. Write an ad they want to respond to.

Most newspapers are full of sterile, traditional, institutional, non-producing ads. What is the purpose of an ad? Make the phone ring, of course. Or drive them to your site. The real estate ad is probably the most misspent item on the broker's budget. They are generally institutional, boring, say-nothing ads that don't generate a response. Here are some samples of some direct response ads:

Some Sample Direct response Ads

Own any home on this page with no down payment! Go to www. prettygoodhomes.com for your free report: How to Buy Any Home up to $700,000 with No Down Payment

Champagne Homes for Beer Budgets

Market correction creates huge opportunity for homebuyers moving up. Save tens of thousands.

Must be sold—many below loan amount. Their loss, your gain. Free info @ www.belowmarket.com

Handyman Special Fixer-Upper

Four homes must sell this weekend

Free info @ www.needtlc.com

Bring Brush, Reap Thousands

Thinking of selling?

Ten things you can do for under $500 total that will put $5,000 or more in your pocket at closing. Go to www.hopetosell.com

Find your next home without an agent

Automated home search sends you a list of homes that fit your criteria, complete with pictures, addresses, and directions. Go to www. losemyhome.com for free report/info.

Own cheaper than rent

Tired of renting? Need a yard for the kids?

Private garage? Indoor laundry? Interest rates make it easy! Bad credit/ no credit no problem. Free report @ www.firsthome.com: How to fire your landlord and own your own home in thirty days.

Here is a test you can run on your ads before you spend money running them in print. Read your ad. If it has vague, ambiguous generalities and platitudes that don't add any value, don't articulate what you do and the benefit to the consumer, don't run it. Read it. If, at the end, you can say, "Well, I would certainly hope so!" do not run it. Example: "I will sell your home for more money." I would certainly hope so. "I will sell your home with the least amount of problems." I would certainly hope so. "I will stay in touch with you during the time we are marketing your home." I would certainly hope so. Get it?

When You Give Me Heat ...

"What happens after they go to the Web site?" Jim asked.

"It depends. If it has what you say in the ad, they will read it. If there is content and information that helps them, and they are interested, they will come back. The consumers don't want to talk to you because they know you are going to try to sell them something. Remember, lifetime value. Educate and serve. Relationships take time. It's a date, not a wedding. Tell them anything and everything they could ever want to know about how to buy, sell, and invest in real estate. You will be perceived as the expert, and when they decide to take the next step, you will be one of the ones they will contact if you have provided pertinent, relevant, no-strings-attached information that helps them in their decision-making process. You must first give in order to receive. Some will take advantage of your kindness and generosity. That is no reason not to be kind and generous. If you want a smile, smile. If you want love, love. If you want to be understood, seek to understand. If you want a lifelong relationship, seek to find out what they want and give it to them freely. Don't be like the guy standing in front of the empty fireplace, screaming, "When you give me heat, I'll give you wood!"

Risk Reversal

At one time or another, each us has most likely bought something and not gotten value for what we paid for. Every time consumers make a decision and prepare to pay for the purchase, they take a risk. Many times, the marketing and sales processes are better than the product itself. The dissatisfied customer has to argue, debate, explain, and go through a series of motions in order to get what he or she wanted and thought he or she was buying. Sometimes he or she never does get the satisfaction he or she was expecting to get from the purchase. Sometimes we, as consumers, are tricked, misled, lied to, and outright swindled, losing both satisfaction and our money.

Marketing campaigns, ads, radio spots, and direct mail pieces that are all the same, proclaiming to be the "cheapest, lowest price, highest quality, best service, fastest delivery," etc., etc., etc. only increase the mistrust consumers have for companies vying for their money. Consumers know that every time they make a purchase, they take a risk. Obviously they are not overly concerned with a piece of bubble gum. Buying a home, on the other hand, is another matter. The higher the price of the item they are considering buying, the higher the risk and, therefore, the greater the fear. If you want to remove the fear, reverse the risk.

Instead of expecting the consumers to overcome their own fears and hesitations and fall so in love with your product or service, or the house you are showing them, that they will say, "What the heck. We'll take it," simply take on the risk for them. Give them a guarantee. Agents have a tough time with this one. They didn't manufacture the product. They don't own it. Sometimes, they don't really know much about it other than the buyer they have with them likes it.

Guarantee it? Excuse me? You want me to what? I know it sounds strange, but think about it. This is going to be one of the biggest financial decisions the buyer or buyers will ever make. This is also going to be one of their biggest risks.

Throw Away the "SOLD" Signs

Are they hesitant, even though they love the home and really want to move? You bet. If this is the right home for them and you know it, are you there to help them make the right decision? Of course. That's why you are there; that is your function; that is what you are paid to do. Agents don't sell houses. No agent ever sold anyone a house. It's just a speech pattern we have.

Actually, they should throw away all the SOLD signs and replace them with signs that are more accurate, signs that say something like, "Chosen by the Smiths, assisted by agent so and so." I never sold anyone a home.

I was with many people when they made the decision to buy one, but I didn't sell it to them. I showed people homes based on their own criteria. I looked at every home on the market in my service area, and when I met someone looking for one, I interviewed him or her intently until I knew before we ever got into the car what he or she was looking for and why he or she was looking for it. I learned early on that I would never sell anyone a home, and I never did.

Instead, I educated them, helped them through the qualifying process, listened to them, and took them to homes they described to me. Then I took away the fear, reversed the risk, and gave them a guarantee. Whether I am representing buyers or sellers, I give a guarantee.

How does it work?

Take Away Their Risk

I represented sellers more than buyers. I will explain why in chapter ten. Sellers, especially sellers who have sold homes before, may have experienced problems with their former agent. Several problems later, they may have decided they chose the wrong agent and tried to cancel the listing, only to learn it was a contract that could not be cancelled without the permission of both parties, and the agent would not release them.

Signing up with any agent now represents a risk for them. What if they choose the wrong one again?

Everything you said in your presentation sounded good to them. You would never do anything to betray their trust, but only you know that. You never really know someone until you either work with them or live with them, and you're not moving in. Are you confident in your ability to service this listing? Is your marketing plan strong? Will you drive traffic to their home? Can you get it sold? Have you told them so? If the answers to these questions are yes, why not back up what you say with a guarantee?

An Example

This is the one I like: I show them my twenty-point marketing plan and tell them this, "If I don't do these twenty things, communicate with you as I do them, and show you I've done them, you can fire me with a phone call. I am not going to ask you to sign an agreement and then disappear behind broken promises. I put it all in writing. Furthermore, if I haven't sold your home in sixty days or less, I will pay you $500.00, and I have put that in writing, too." See how different this is? Instead of expecting them to trust us and take a risk, we reverse the risk. We take the risk by giving them a way out if we don't perform, and we earn their trust over time.

Are you different from the average agent? Are you better than the average agent? Then you have to say and do things differently. Otherwise, in the eyes of the consumer, you are the same.

The $500.00 guarantee does two things: It keeps you from taking overpriced listings, one of the most vexing problems of the industry, and it shows the seller you are willing to back up your words with actions. You may be thinking, "What!? What if I have to pay it? I can't afford to pay them $500.00!" First of all, if you can't get the home sold in sixty days, you may want to take a good hard look at your marketing plan or your pricing plan, because the home is either under-marketed or overpriced.

Second, you don't pay them in cash, you credit them at closing. It is stated right there in the guarantee certificate you give them. Last, what if the home did not sell, and you did pay them $500.00? What better marketing event could there possibly be? Call the news stations and hold a press conference! Have one of those great big checks printed up and deliver it to them, take pictures, and send them to the newspapers, even create marketing flyers about it. "Agent pays seller $500.00. Home didn't sell." Do you know how much money that will make you? What I'm saying is, think of ways you can make these ideas work instead of ways they won't.

If you are representing the buyer, you can use it like this: "If you decide for any reason in the first year that the home is not for you and decide to sell, I will list it with no listing commission." If that helped people get over their fear and allowed you to close ten more deals per year, and you made $5,000 per deal, that's an extra $50,000 in income.

Is there a downside to this offer? Of course there is, and you are the one taking some risk. What if two of the ten took you up on your offer? What would that mean? Let's look at it in more detail.

You list the two houses, agreeing to pay a selling commission, but charging no listing commission. Suppose it cost you $2,000 to market the two properties. You now have an extra two listings in your inventory and, from those lawn signs you picked up, three new buyers, two of which bought from you. That's two transactions you otherwise would not have. At $5,000 per transaction (example only—commissions and agent/broker commission splits vary), that's another $10,000 in revenue you generated, simply by reversing the risk and backing it up with a guarantee. Subtract the $2,000 for marketing, and you net $8,000. Not to mention the referrals.

Then create a marketing piece out of that and tell everyone in your database and on your direct mail list that you did it and why. "I listed my client's home free!" Remember the tenets of marketing. Have something good to say, say it well, say it often. You want to build trust. Give your customers a guarantee, fulfill it, and then tell everyone how you keep your word even when you have to write a check.

Back End

Earlier, I wrote about determining the lifetime value of the customer. Since the average homeowner moves every five to seven years, waiting for him or her to buy again may not be such a great idea. Therefore, although the homeowners may not be candidates for a while, they know people who are. Exceed their expectations and ask for referrals. If you go above and beyond the call of duty and constantly wow them with your service, they will be happy to help you by referring their friends, business associates, and family members to you.

I wrote earlier that the average lifetime value of the pizza eater was $1,200, and that of the Cadillac buyer was $300,000. If your profit on a pizza was $6, would you give up the profit on the first one to obtain that customer for life? Would you spend $6 to get a $1,200 customer? Of course you would. You give up a little on the front end to make it on the back end. You give your current customers a price break in order to get a chance to work with them so they can refer people to you. This can come in a number of ways. If you have their home listed, and they are local move-up buyers, you have two transactions that you will be paid on. Give them a gift certificate at a local furniture store, hardware store, or garden center that's valid upon the closing of the second transaction. Reduce the price of their home by a few percentage points by shaving your fee if they use you for both transactions. Get concessions from the title company and lender.

If you are doing a decent volume, get them to waive their junk fees and pass that savings on to the client.

There are many marketing techniques and tools that will get your message across. By determining the lifetime value of your customer, you will begin to see it may be better to focus and develop a target market built on referrals than to try to be all things to everyone. Developing your unique marketing position and utilizing direct response ads, risk reversal, and the back end, combined with business cards, flyers, a newsletter, postcards, and a content-rich Web site will be an ongoing process that, if done well and measured accurately, will turn your business into a lead-generating machine. It will produce an endless stream of thankful, educated, highly qualified, and willing prospects.

A good marketing program makes the sale easy.

A poor marketing plan makes the sale hard.

TESTIMONIALS

"Best course I've ever taken—all this is not taught in any school. Thanks! I'll recommend highly!!"
Diana Brown

★ ★ ★ ★ ★ ★ ★ ★ ★ ★ ★ ★ ★ ★ ★ ★ ★ ★ ★ ★

"Thank you, Wayne! You've given me the tools to my financial independence in the most powerful, entertaining, and heartfelt way."
Josephine Cordova

★ ★ ★ ★ ★ ★ ★ ★ ★ ★ ★ ★ ★ ★ ★ ★ ★ ★ ★ ★

"Should be mandatory for all new agents. Helps a new agent understand the motivation for a buyer and then build their own wealth. Great job."
H.D. McFarland

★ ★ ★ ★ ★ ★ ★ ★ ★ ★ ★ ★ ★ ★ ★ ★ ★ ★

"Excellent course. Recommend to everyone. As usual, very enlightening."
Thelma Sorgman

★ ★ ★ ★ ★ ★ ★ ★ ★ ★ ★ ★ ★ ★ ★ ★ ★ ★ ★ ★

"I have learned more in your 2 classes than I have learned in my entire education. Thanks a million."
Travis Mathews

Chapter Eight

Sales: It's All About the Relationship

Now that you are face-to-face, how do you go about asking for the business?

There are only three basic things you need to know about sales:

1. How to ask high quality questions
2. The four different personality types
3. The three different modalities

(But first you have to get your mindset right.)

Just as in other aspects of the business-building process, the sales process has more than one part to it and consists of many parts working in harmony and conjunction with each other.

Do This Exercise Now:

Get a clean sheet of paper and write down the first *ten* words that come into your mind when you think of the word *salesman*.

How many negative words are on your list?

Most people have a negative impression of salespeople. They see them as pushy, self-centered, obnoxious, commission-grabbing hucksters. Then, when the salespeople find themselves at the moment of truth, when they need to help the buyer or seller make a decision, they fail to respond in a positive way because they don't want to be seen as pushy, obnoxious, arrogant commission grabbers. Somehow, agents have it wired up in their heads that asking questions equates with being pushy. Nothing could be further from the truth. In fact, just the opposite is true. Asking clear, concise questions in an interview process in order to determine what the prospect's wants and needs are, is the highest value you can bring to the transaction.

To do so any other way is an invalidation of the prospect and a complete and total waste of time. To go on a listing presentation and give advice without knowing the seller's motivations, situation, time frame, goals, and objectives is not only in astonishingly poor taste, it is amateurish and unprofessional at best.

To put a buyer in your car and drag him or her all over town from subdivision to subdivision without a clue of what he or she is looking for as far as employment, schools, religious centers, etc., waiting for him or her to say, "Stop! I'll take this one," is not going to work.

The Problem Is the Paradox

What is a paradox? The definition is: what you avoid, you get.

What do agents want to avoid? They want to avoid losing the buyer. What do they do? Answer the telephone and tell the caller everything about the home, describing it from end to end and top to bottom. They rarely ask for a name or a number or ask what the buyer wants or needs for fear of losing them. This only results in losing them.

It happens way too often—all because of the thought that asking questions equals pushy. No one wants to be seen as pushy. It's only natural as humans that we desire to have others like us, respect us, and have good things to say about us. Agents who don't ask questions for fear of losing prospects are losing prospects. As a salesperson, you are doing one of two things: **You are either asking questions, or you are making assumptions.**

I set up a live telephone in the marketing class I teach, and we call the top ten real estate brokers in town, just for edification. I pose as a cash buyer in many different price ranges, asking many questions about the house advertised in the paper. The agent answers all my questions, asking me none. Then I tell the agent I am new to town, need to make a decision quickly, and I have a map and need to drive by the house. The agent gives me directions. I say I hope I can find it. The agent wishes me good luck.

The following is a true story. The names have been changed to protect the guilty.

I was in Bloomington, Indiana, getting my son squared away at Indiana University. We were returning to his apartment after doing some extensive food shopping when we passed two beautiful homes side by side with "For Sale" signs in the yards, just one block from campus. My wife automatically grabbed her cell phone out of her purse and started dialing the 812 area code.

"Did you get it?" she asked.

"Of course," I replied, and I then proceeded to give her the agent's phone number without even slowing down.

In fifteen seconds, we had the office on the phone. We began qualifying the property. Got it? WE began qualifying THEM.

We asked the typical questions investors ask:

How much are they asking?

What are the rents?

If vacant, what could we get for rent?

What is the zoning?

How many students will it accommodate?

What financing, if any, is being offered?

What is the cash-on-cash return?

What is the cap rate?

Can you send me a proforma?

We discovered the typical things.

They were asking $295,000 for one house, $475,000 for the other.

They were vacant, no idea what rents could be, no idea what the zoning was or how many students they would accommodate, nothing about financing, and as to the proforma question, we got the usual, "Huh?"

The assistant asked if we wanted to speak to the listing agent. We said yes, and he called back within fifteen minutes, offering to show the property.

We arrived a short time later and began determining how the property could best be utilized.

I asked him to tell me the story of the property.

He told me the houses had belonged to two sisters who had both passed away and that it was an estate sale. It had been on the market all summer, approximately 126 days, with lots of showings but no offers.

I asked him what the zoning was. He didn't know.

The house could easily accommodate twelve to fourteen students. I asked him if the zoning restrictions allowed ten. He said the restrictions would only allow three.

I was incredulous. "Three? It has FOUR bedrooms!" He said that, according to the city, three tenants were the most I could put in there. I asked him what the rents would be.

"About $450 each," he said.

A quick calculation will tell you that even if you were foolish enough to put 20 percent down, three students at $450 each would not begin to cover the debt, much less ongoing expenses.

"Those numbers don't work," I said.

"I know. I've been telling the seller we need to reduce the price."

He mumbled something about having dinner the night before with the soon-to-be mayor. He talked about the fact that the houses were built in 1886 and had basements, and he went on and on about the iron fence in the front yard and what great fence makers they were back then and how the city had to put up a huge marker sign in front of the house because people sometimes had a tendency to run through the stop sign and, as he put it, "pay uninvited visits," ending up in the front yard.

He mentioned the street had been widened over the years and that was why it was so close to the house. I didn't care anything about the mayor-to-be, the fence, the proximity of the road, or anything else he thought was important. I ultimately wanted to know whether this would make a good investment or not.

We walked through the second house. He chatted. He talked. My wife and I looked, trying to figure out how to make the deal work. The floor plan just did not work. All the bedrooms were upstairs, which left most of the downstairs, half the house, as wasted space.

He went on and on about the fireplace, the patios, the deck, and the poplar floors. He told us the house had not been updated since the sixties, and there was current obvious water damage throughout the house.

Even though the roof was leaking and the walls were peeling, none of these things bothered me. I like fixer-uppers, yet the agent never even asked me if I liked fixer-uppers. He never asked me anything about what I was looking for in an investment property. He just proceeded to tell us all the negative aspects about the property. It was like he was trying to talk us out of buying it, while we were trying to figure out how to make it work. He not only failed to show the way the deal could work, he actually got in the way. We could barely look at the place because he followed us from room to room, chatting away about this and that. While we were looking and thinking, he was walking and talking, totally oblivious to what we were wanting to accomplish.

We were figuring our return. Unfortunately, there was just no way to convert that floor plan to multi-family use. Plus, it needed about $200,000 in repairs and remodeling. It was not going to work for us for multi-family use, which we were able to determine in about twenty minutes. It was definitely for an owner-occupant, and I am not moving to Bloomington. (Not that there is anything wrong with Bloomington; it's actually a quaint little college town. Moving just isn't in the plans.)

We then proceeded to view the other property. It had a floor plan that lent itself to multi-family use. The four bedrooms were large, separated from each other with shared bathrooms. There was additional space that could be a fifth bedroom, and there was a great room for socializing and television and two large dining areas. I said to him, "There has to be a way to increase the density. With this proximity to the university, I find it hard to believe that the city would limit a four-bedroom house to only three people. It doesn't make sense. There has to be a loophole somewhere. What can we do to get the occupancy to ten? At ten, the numbers work."

That's when he said it. "That's what other people have said. I had an idea about that. You could apply for a boarding house permit. I know someone who had this same problem, and they were able to do it that way."

My jaw dropped. Why? My jaw dropped because he knew someone who had the same problem, and yet he did nothing to remedy the problem. In essence, buyers who had seen the property had said, "If you fix this problem, I'll buy it." He failed to do anything about it. I was stunned.

Your job as business owners is to find the problems people are having and solve them, not tell them what the problems are and hope that they somehow are fixed on their own.

Then the weather turned bad. It began to rain quite heavily. I needed to get to Indianapolis and return the rental car. I needed to catch a flight home. I needed to get my son back to his apartment. I needed some answers.

I needed a Realtor® who knew how to do his or her job and best serve me.

Then he did it. He turned to my son and said, "You probably never get into trouble. But, if you do, here is my card. Call me anytime. I'm happy to help any way I can."

This display of kindness and generosity typifies the typical Realtor®. Most everyone I know enters the business because they like to help other people. There is a lot of personal satisfaction in helping people sell and buy homes and seeing the joy and excitement that people experience. I saw a quote once that goes like this:

"Real estate is the best business in the world. We make other people's dreams come true ... while achieving our own."

So, what went wrong, and why do so many fail?

It all begins with a thought.

The diagram below illustrates what usually happens in any given situation.

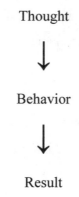

Everything begins with a thought. The thought drives us to do something, which is our behavior. How we behave, ***what we do***, determines our results. If you want to change the result, change the thought.

This is why most educational, training programs and seminars don't work long-term. They focus on the person's behavior. Our seminars focus on the thought that drives the behavior. The reason people behave the way they do is because they have a thought that behaving in such a manner will get them what they want.

Often, people will hold a thought and continue the unproductive behavior even though it doesn't work. Even though they are not getting what they want and even when they do not achieve their intended result, they persist in maintaining the same behavior.

That is how powerful our thoughts and the subconscious mind can be. The subconscious mind is the most sensitive instrument in the universe, and it will behave in accordance with what it believes.

This wonderful man, who is well educated, cordial, pleasant, well meaning, kind, and helpful, holds a thought that is keeping him from doing what needs to be done.

It is keeping him from properly representing his client (the seller).
It is keeping him from providing excellent service to his customers (the buyer).
It is keeping the property on the market longer than it should be.
It is keeping him from making lots of money.
It is keeping him from building a referral-based business.

> *This is the thought that is in his way and keeping him from building his business. He thinks that asking questions is equivalent to being "pushy," and he does not want to be seen as a "pushy salesman."*

Nothing could be further from the truth. Go back to the exercise I asked you to do at the beginning of this chapter. Tell yourself the truth. What do you think of when you hear the word *salesman*? What image or picture pops into your mind? Describe that image in detail. Write down all the words you associate with *salesman* and read your list again.

These are the thoughts that dictate your behavior. If you think salespeople are (insert the negative words from your list here), you will find it very tough to sell, because your behavior will drive you to do things to keep you from being seen that way.

Ideal Scene

This is the step-by-step process of how this property showing (Bloomington, Indiana) could have been handled more effectively.

First of all, there is a market for every house. The question is: What is the market for this house? Look at the house. What is the profile of the potential buyer? Once you know, you can market directly to that group.

For example, young parents who are planning on growing their families will probably not be prospects for a home with what we call a "mother-in-law" (MIL) floor plan or a two-story plan. The MIL plan is where the master bedroom is on one side of the house, and the rest of the bedrooms are on the other side, separated from each other by the kitchen and living and dining areas.

Parents with babies and young children are usually going to want them close by, initially sharing their own room and eventually moving them into the adjoining room, so they can closely monitor them and be with them.

As the kids grow up, the MIL or a two-story plan may be more advantageous, if nothing else but for the noise factor. Now you'll see that the parents want space away from the kids and vice versa. This arrangement also works well for "empty nesters," couples whose children have grown and left home. The separation works well in giving owners and guests privacy. You may also find that seniors would probably shy away from two-story plans, choosing to not navigate stairs.

Now, let us revisit the Bloomington, Indiana, story. So, here are these two houses just a few blocks from the university of 40,000 or so students. What is the target market? Quite possibly an investor. Now that we know what our market is, we prepare to market and sell to that market.

(Q)   How do we market to them?

(A)   We use all the marketing tools available to us as Realtors®; MLS, newspaper ads, the Internet, direct mail, flyers, lawn signs (which is how I found it), etc.

(Q)   How do we sell it?

(A)   We prepare for the investor to show up.

(Q)   What is an investor interested in?

(A)   We don't know yet. Some buy for appreciation; some buy for cash flow; some buy based on an IRR, or Internal Rate of Return; some buy based on a capitalization, or "cap," rate; some only want pristine Class A properties; some like fixer-uppers; and on it goes.

How can we find out what they want? How do we find out what any homebuyer wants? Sounds elementary, doesn't it?

This is the main reason most people who are in sales—not just real estate but salespeople everywhere—fail. They do not know how to ask high quality questions. They think in the deep recesses of their minds that asking questions equals being a pushy salesman.

They don't go through the discovery of wants and needs process.

Stop Showing It and Start Selling It

Again, the reason I was so surprised at this listing agent's behavior is because he said he had heard the same comments that the occupancy load was too restrictive and would not produce a decent return, yet he did nothing. When the market talks to you, listen and act. You cannot bend the market to your will. Our job as businesspeople is to find out what the market wants. If the market says, "I want more density," your job is to go get more density.

He also said he had dinner the night before with the soon-to-be mayor, yet he knew nothing about the boarding house application/licensing process. What a great source of information: the incoming mayor. All the listing agent had to do was ask the mayor-to-be who to talk to and then go find out everything about the process. Anticipate your potential investor and get all the documents necessary to give him or her when he or she shows up.

You'll then want to prepare the proforma. Ask the following questions.

1. What are you looking for in an investment property?

2. Are you interested in your IRR, cap rate, or cash-on-cash return?

3. Will you be financing the purchase or paying cash?

4. When you invest, do you prefer to put a sizable amount down or leverage the financing as much as possible?

5. Do you need assistance with financing, or do you already have a lender? (This would have been particularly helpful to me since I was from out of state. This is why I emphasize assembling your team in chapter five). Phrase it like this: "Your finances are your own private matter, of course, and I am sure qualifying for the financing won't be a problem. However, before the seller will remove the property from the marketplace, he or she will want some kind of assurance that the prospective borrower is qualified. Here is a list of three lenders I know who have expressed an interest in providing financing on this property if you would like to give them a call. I can assure you that your conversations with them will be kept confidential." Then give the prospect the list.

6. This one needs a little TLC; is that okay? (if applicable)

7. This one is a major fixer-upper; is that okay? (if applicable) (Note: There is no need to sugarcoat it. Describe the property AS IT IS. As I wrote earlier, there is a market for every property. Some agents get too far into what I call "creative marketing" when describing their listings, and when I go see them, sometimes they are nothing like what they were described to be. If it's a fixer-upper, do not say it "shows like a model." Just market it to the fixer-upper market. When you market the right product to the right market, the right buyers show up.)

8. Will this property fit into your portfolio?

9. Will you be converting any other of your investments to acquire this one?

10. What information can I provide you with?

11. May I (show) send you a proforma?

   ***Last but not least: the high quality trial close question:

12. If I could show you how you could do everything you've told me, what do you think your time frame to make a decision might be?

Now, what have we done? We prepared. We asked high quality questions that qualify the buyer as to a time frame, and we built credibility by demonstrating our ability to handle the deal.

With this process in place, we are now ready. We have the documentation from the city on the zoning. We are educated regarding the boarding license process. We have contacts we can provide—actual names and numbers of people we have spoken to that we can give to the investor. We have the proforma showing the rates of return. We have a list of engaging, high quality, discovery-of-wants-and-needs questions.

We also have an intelligent report for our client, the seller. As it stands now, when the listing agent calls his seller to give him or her the weekly update on the activity on the property, what is he going to say? "It's priced too high."

With the process outlined here, the agent is much more prepared to report to the client. "They are experienced investors who are highly qualified to make the purchase. Unfortunately, as it is currently priced, the returns simply are not there. Since we have been at this price for four months now and have had no offers despite multiple showings, I would suggest pricing it more in line with investor expectations in order to attract an offer."

(Note: Sellers often set the price of their property based on one of these five things: their emotion, what they have in it as far as improvements, what they initially paid for it, what the neighbors are asking for their property, or their opinion of what they think it is worth. When you use a proforma when listing an investment property, the return, which is the ONLY reason the investor is buying, sets the price. It reduces all the opinions of the seller and instead uses factual numbers to set the price realistically in line with the market.)

Agents Will Flow Like Water to the Easiest Deal

The most important thing about this aforementioned process is that we made it easy for people do buy your listings. As a Realtor®, that is your job. Don't make the buyers do all the work. Don't make the buyer's agent do all the work. Don't make the investor do all the work. You do all the work.

Make your listings easy to sell, and you will sell more listings. Sell more listings, and you will get more listings. Get more listings, and you will attract more buyers.

Your job is to solve the problem. The bigger the problem, the bigger the check. That's why CEOs make more money than secretaries. They solve bigger problems.

As I was driving to the airport after dropping my son off and saying our goodbyes, the listing agent called me on my cell phone.

"Hey, Wayne," he said. "Can I get your e-mail address? I want to send you some pictures of the house."

Was he lazy? No. Was his follow-up good? Yes. Did he mean well? Yes. Was he doing his best? Yes.

What he still didn't understand was that I didn't want or need pictures of the house. I JUST SAW IT.

What I needed was a proforma showing my return (which I can do in about twenty minutes; it's no big deal, but it would have been nice to have had one handed to me) and a solution to the problem of increasing the density.

If I can increase density by putting more students in the building, it increases the rental income, thereby increasing my return, at which time I am more inclined to buy.

I may not do any business with this agent. However, he did volunteer to help out my son if he got into trouble, and for that I am grateful. And that is what is heartbreaking about the real estate business and the training that goes with it. Here is this kind, generous, well-meaning person who obviously cares about other people, but he doesn't know how to really serve—all because of the thought, "Asking questions is being nosy and pushy. Salesmen are low lifes." You serve by discovering wants and needs.

The Solution
This Is the Five-Step Process

1.   Discover wants and needs by asking high quality questions.
2.   Find the problem.
3.   Educate and inform the prospect.
4.   Provide answers, options, and solutions.
5.   Ask for a time frame for a decision.

Like anything else, your results are determined by your attitude and your point of view.

If you think salespeople are low-life dirtbags only out to make money by tricking and deceiving people, your attitude toward salespeople will be negative.

Your attitude toward yourself as a salesperson will be negative as well, and your results will suffer. What is your attitude toward salespeople? How do you see yourself as a salesperson? How do you think others see you?

People LOVE to Be Sold

This has always been my attitude. I have been selling professionally since I was sixteen years old. I believe salespeople offer a valuable service to others. We wouldn't have all the selections, options, and choices if a salesperson hadn't sold that product to the store where we can buy it. I love salespeople, and people LOVE to be sold! What people don't like is to be deceived, misled, or cheated. Somehow, this became selling. It's not selling; it's deceiving, misleading, and cheating.

The marketing got me to go to the hardware store in search of ceiling fans, the electronics store in search of a phone, and the superstore in search of shoes. So, the marketing dollars worked. They got me in the door. Now comes the sale.

We Have Too Much

If ever there were a need for good salespeople, it's now. There are so many choices and so many options and so much merchandise that we can barely get through the stores. Someone who can ask specific questions and determine wants and needs quickly and make recommendations based on thorough knowledge of the product, is a very valuable person.

What Is a Sale?

What is a sale? It is choice plus exchange. If there is no choice, it's a monopoly. If there is no exchange, it's theft. You must have both elements: choice and exchange. Do we have choices? Absolutely. I am as confused as ever about what to buy. Will there be an exchange? There will be if someone sells me what I want, which is what I want. I want someone to care enough about me and my problems and my time to come over and ask me some really good, high quality questions to determine what I want and what I need. Based on their product knowledge, they can give me some options, let me decide, take my money, and let me get on with my life and not leave me standing there in the aisle wondering why there are so many different kinds of everything.

This would be the ideal scenario:

"What brings you to our store today?"

"I need three ceiling fans."

"Great. We have many to choose from. Do you have a budget or price in mind?"

"It's for rental houses I'm remodeling. Probably something mid-range. Something durable, but not top of the line."

"Does it matter to you if it has four or five blades?"

"No."

"Do you want the reversible feature?"

"Sure."

"We have polished brass, antique brass, white, or wood. What color scheme is the interior?"

"Two are white, and one has wood paneling. So, two white and one wood."

"Would you like them with light kits included?"

"Sure."

"Great. I recommend you get these two and this one. They are on sale, have a one-year warranty, are from a reputable manufacturer, are good quality, and will look like you spent a lot of money on them. Will there be anything else today?"

I am ecstatic. This is just what I want.

"No," I say, smiling. I am happy now.

"How about light bulbs?" he asks me.

> I forgot all about light bulbs. Am I glad he asked? Absolutely. He saved me a trip back to the store that I didn't want to go to in the first place.
>
> "Good idea. I didn't even think about bulbs. Thank you for reminding me."
>
> He says, "No problem; that's what we're here for. Will that be all today?"
>
> "Yep, I think that's it."
>
> "MasterCard or Visa?"

Now we're done, and I am out of there. I wish every shopping experience went that way.

Do you see the difference between this and the typical "can I help you?" question most clerks ask? That question is almost always followed by, "No, I'm just looking." The reason is because it is a poor quality question.

The clerk at the home store took the time to ask me a series of high quality questions, determine my wants and needs, make a recommendation, and upsell me on the bulbs. Did I love being sold? Absolutely! Do I go back there time and again? Absolutely. Am I a referring client?

You bet.

The Key to Becoming a Professional Salesperson

You have to care more about the customer than you do yourself. You may want to read that sentence again. If you are more concerned about what the customer thinks of you, you care about you, not them. If your desire is to be liked, you care about you, not them. I don't care if they like me. I care if they get the truth. I care if they get good service. I care if their dreams come true. Their liking me is secondary. Giving them good, sound counsel from my experience even though it may not be what they want to hear is what gets the referrals. My clients know that I will tell them the truth, even if it is contradictory to what they think or know or even want to hear.

This is one of the reasons there are so many overpriced listings in the marketplace.

Agents are afraid to tell the sellers what their home is really worth because they want to be liked. Is it the agents' fault the seller bought at the top of the market? Is it the agents' fault the market has slowed down and the sellers need to sell? Is it the agents' fault the seller owes more on the home than it is worth? Of course not.

This is the power of the paradox. The agent is afraid the seller will get upset or not like him or her if he or she tells the seller that the asking price is way too high. The agent takes the listing at a price so far above the market the home has no chance of selling. The home sits on the market for several months, putting the sellers in a financial jam. Now the sellers really are upset, and they do not like their agent, blaming him or her because the home hasn't sold.

Three Tools for Asking High quality Questions

That is why I like to use tried-and-true methods that get results. The next three tools are tools that I have found useful over the years. I hesitated to mention them at first because they have been around for so long and are somewhat dated; however, my observation has been that very few salespeople have truly mastered the art of asking questions. So, at the risk of being redundant, I feel these tools are worth mentioning again. I have been using these tools for years and continue to get good results with them.

1. The Porcupine

The porcupine is a tool that keeps salespeople from making a costly error: making assumptions. See, when a buyer asks, "Does it have a big yard?" what do we automatically assume? He or she wants a big yard. He or she may want the opposite.

The untrained amateur says, "Yes, it does. It is one of the largest yards in the area," thinking this is what the buyer wants and that he or she is about to get a sale. Adrenalin flows. Blood pumps. Heart beats fast.

Buyer says, "That's too bad. I'm sick of all the yard work. That's one of the reasons we're moving. I want a small yard." Adrenalin stops flowing. Blood pressure returns to normal. Heart slows. Uncertainty sets in. Agent tries to undo the damage.

"Well, it's not that big. Most of it is rock and cliff, so there is not that much grass, actually. The actual yard part is really kind of small."

The confidence gap widens, the trust goes down, the buyer feels the salesperson is being less than truthful, and the conversation ends.

The pro, on the other hand, asks, "Did you want a big yard?" The buyer says, "No. I'm sick of all the yard work. That's one of the reasons we're moving." The pro says, "Great! May I just ask you a few quick questions to see if maybe this home might be one you want to see?" and goes on to have a conversation with the buyer, building trust, asking questions, interviewing, qualifying, and closing the confidence gap.

Porcupine: Always answer a question with a question.

2. Alternate Choice

The second tool for asking questions is the alternate choice. The alternate choice is a question with two answers. Either one is a yes. It works by giving the borrower a choice by asking either/or questions. If the buyer says, "What kind of financing is available?" the salesperson responds with, "Down payments are flexible. Did you want to put down 5 percent or 10 percent?" If the buyer says 5 percent, they've said, "Yes, I'm going ahead." The salesperson might ask another question such as, "Did you want to take possession at the beginning of the month or at the end?" If the buyer says, "At the end," they've said yes. If you're walking through the house with them and you ask, "Would this be your son's room or your daughter's room?" and they say, "My son's; we want him close by so that we can keep an eye on him." They've said yes. These are all examples of using questions with alternate choice, which is a question with two answers. When they answer, they have said yes, and they are ready to move forward.

Alternate choice: A question with two answers. Either one is a yes.

3. The Tie-Down

The third tool is called a tie-down. A tie-down is a question at the end of a sentence that requires an answer—phrases like, "isn't it?" "doesn't it?" "aren't they?" and "don't they?" All of these are examples of tie-downs, aren't they? When you use them at the end of a sentence, they turn the sentence into a question, don't they? I'm using them now, aren't I? You want me to stop, don't you? I'm not going to, am I? All of those are tie-downs, and the key to using them is to look for a positive statement from the buyer first.

Never tie down a negative; always tie down a positive. If the buyer says something positive, tie it down. If you're on a listing presentation that is scheduled for seven o'clock, and you show up at seven o'clock, they may answer the door and say, "You're right on time." Is that a positive comment? Yes. Tie it down. You might say, "Being on time shows respect and professionalism, don't you agree?" Then as you sit down at the table to begin your presentation, they might say, "I've heard good things about your company." Is that a positive comment? You bet. Tie it down. "Having a good reputation in the community is important, isn't it?" As you go through the presentation, they might say, "Your information is very detailed." You want to tie that down. "You want someone who pays attention to detail, don't you?"

Every time you hear a positive comment, tie it down, and then later you'll come back and remind them of all the things that were positive.

If they don't make a positive comment, you can always elicit one. You can show them your marketing plan, and after you've explained all the points of it and all the pieces that fit together, just ask them, "You do want your home to have maximum exposure, don't you?"

The purpose of a tie-down is to highlight and accentuate the positive aspects of doing business with you, and everything about your marketing, follow-up, etc. that is going to make a difference to the prospect. If you tell them those things, they may not believe them, but if you ask them and they agree, then it makes it more believable to them. Remember, the key is to look for a positive comment. If they look at your marketing plan and say, "Our neighbor's house didn't sell for that much," don't look at it and say, "It didn't sell for that much, did it?" They'll say, "Your information is wrong, isn't it? That's why we're not going to use you, are we? It's time for you to go, isn't it?"

Interested Versus Interesting

There is an old saying that goes, "Telling isn't selling," and it is so true. Yet today, most salespeople try to talk their clients into buying. Salespeople are either being interested or interesting. The interested ones are asking high quality questions aimed at determining the prospect's wants and needs so they can get on with providing the information, education, and advice the prospect requires to make an informed decision. The interesting ones are talking, talking, talking, hoping and trying to be interesting enough that the prospect will want to know more. Learning how to ask high quality questions is an art form. If a salesperson can just master the art of asking questions, his or her income will make a quantum leap. Combine that with a thorough understanding of the personality types and the three basic modalities, and your sales go exponential while your problems drop off to practically zero.

Napolean Hill wrote in *Think and Grow Rich*, "It is as useless to try to sell a man something until you have first made him want to listen as it would be to command the earth to stop rotating."

Your Income Is in Direct Proportion to the Quality of Your Questions

The better the question, the more money you will make. In school, we are taught to have the right answers. In business, you must have the right questions.

Train Your Brain

Train your brain to speak only in questions. When someone asks you a question, answer it with a question. Practice this over and over until asking questions becomes an integral part of who you are and what you do, until you do it automatically and without thinking. Stop the habit of answering questions and begin the habit of asking them. Results are all about habits. Oversleeping, overeating, overdrinking, and smoking are bad habits.

Improve habits and life improves. Asking questions is a great habit. Gather as much information as you can. Only then can you solve problems and make recommendations based on what is best for all parties. Sometimes my wife and I will carry on a conversation and never make a statement. Here is an example of a recent conversation we had:

Lynn: Are you going in for the meeting today?

Wayne: Is that meeting today? It's Tuesday already?

L: Time flies, doesn't it? Didn't you get my memo?

W: When did you send it?

L: Have you checked your e-mail lately?

W: Didn't we have this conversation yesterday?

L: Aren't you pleased I reminded you?

W: Is it still at ten?

L: Isn't that the usual time we meet?

(Pause)

L: Do you know where we're meeting?

W: At the hotel down from the seafood restaurant?

L: What are you doing afterward?

W: You want to have lunch?

L: What would you like to have?

W: How about the café on the corner with the Italian umbrellas?

L: Can we get a table?

W: How should I know? You want to try?

L: What have we got to lose?

W: So, we'll meet there after the meeting, or should we ride together?

L: Why don't you follow me?

W: Do you remember where it is?

L: Have I ever forgotten?

This may seem a little extreme, but I assure you, it is not atypical of our conversations. Having two salespeople under the same roof can be challenging. Sometimes I don't know who's selling whom.

Twenty Questions You Should Ask Every Seller Before You Ever Go on the Listing Presentation

1. Where are you moving?

2. Why are you moving?

3. How much are you asking for your home?

   If they give you a price, ask:

4. Do you mind if I ask where you got the price?

   If they don't have a price, ask:

5. Have you had an appraisal done?

   If yes—What did it show as the value?

   If no—Are you looking for me to provide that data?

6. Do you have a number you need to reach in order to make the move?

7. Do you know the tax assessed value?

8. How much do you expect to net from the sale?

9. What is your time frame?

10. How many agents are you interviewing?

11. Is experience important to you?

12. Are you willing to do minor cosmetic improvements if it will help the home sell for more money?

13. Who else will be involved in the decision?

14. What will you do if the home doesn't sell?

15. Do you want me to provide you with a thirty-, sixty-, or ninety-day price range?

16. What are you looking for in an agent?

17. What are your goals in selling?

18. Anything else?

19. Would you like to get back together tomorrow or the day after?

20. Is there anything else you think I should know?

Selling is not making the decision for your client so you can get paid. Selling is servicing the prospect, helping, inquiring, educating, informing, giving options, and asking the client what he or she prefers. The number one job of a salesperson is to find out what is wanted and needed and then provide it.

When an agent sits down with a prospect and asks a series of well-thought-out questions that are specifically designed to determine wants and needs, and they are sincere and coming from service, the prospects notice and feel the difference. They open up, and they talk. Ask the same question many times until you are very clear about their goals, desires, and dreams. Remember, we are making dreams come true here! Get clear on their dreams, and make them come true for them. When you come from that place as you interview and listen sincerely and intently, your prospect will become a loyal and ultimately fanatical client, referring many others to you. Why? Because you put them first, you asked high quality questions, you listened, and you made it happen.

High quality questions are designed to determine wants and needs. Be specific and ask: when? where? why? how? what?

Low quality questions are those designed to trick prospects into saying yes.

If you could save money, you would want to, wouldn't you?

If I could get you a good deal, would you be interested?

Of course they are going to say yes to these questions. People want to save money, and people want a good deal.

Questions like these, with obvious "yes" answers, do nothing to build trust or bridge the confidence gap. They are invalidating and insulting to the prospect.

How do you get everything in this world you could ever possibly want? Simply ask. I have made some of my biggest sales and best investments just by asking for what I wanted.
My wife and I own a home that appraised for $650,000 that we bought for $135,000. How? I just asked.

We bought a sixteen-unit building in downtown Austin for $3,000 down, owner-financed, with no payments for the first nine months. How? We just asked.

We bought a business for $10,000 down, owner-financed, that throws off $1,000,000 per year in cash flow. How? We just asked.

I could go on and on. I hope I don't sound like I am bragging. It's just amazing what you can achieve just by asking for what you want. Whether I am selling or buying, I am always asking lots of questions.

Ten Steps to Getting What You Want

1.   Ask someone who can help, meaning owners, managers, supervisors, etc.

2.   Ask someone who can make the decision. Always talk to the person who has the authority to make the decision.

3.   Ask who will be involved in making the decision. Is there a husband, wife, sister, brother, boss, buyer, or someone you have not met who will decide or help decide? Find out.

4.   Ask clearly.

5.   State what is in it for them.

6.   Ask as many times as it takes.

7.   Ask differently each time.

8.   Ask what it would take for it to happen.

9.   Ask what they would do if they were you.

10.   Go up the ladder.

What I mean by the last one is to keep going to higher and higher levels of authority, always being polite and courteous, yet at the same time firm and resolute. Remember—the goal is to get to the boss and everyone has one.

There is an old saying: "If you want to know why John Smith buys what John Smith buys, you need to see the world through John Smith's eyes."

Different Strokes ...

"I've been on several listing presentations," said Bill. "I can't get sellers to list with me. What would you advise?"

"I would begin with a thorough understanding of my audience. What type of person are you presenting to? My father used to say to me, 'It would be a dull world if we were all the same.' Since we are not, an understanding of why people say what they say, do what they do, and do it the way they do it, makes all the difference in the world. With this understanding, you can predict with 95 percent certainty (or more) what people are going to do, or say, as well as why and when they will do it or say it. You can predict their behavior with a high degree of accuracy."

"You can?" Jim asked, sure that I was pulling Bill's leg.

"Sure," I assured him. "It's easy. Everyone has patterns, natural tendencies, particular and specific ways of behaving. Once you understand the patterns and can recognize them, you can predict what they will do in certain situations. You can also predict what they will say and how they will say it. There are four basic personality styles, according to Inscape Publishing, the provider of the DISC Personality Profile system.

"The personality styles are dominant, influencing, steady, and conscientious. We have been using this product for years, and it has proven to be of tremendous value. We have benefited from its use in our hiring processes, our marketing efforts, sales, negotiations, and our overall general communication. Our business efficiency has improved greatly from the use of this information. As we understand more about others, we begin to understand more about ourselves. This understanding has taken our relationships with others, and even each other, to a whole new level."

Dominant

"The Dominant, or "D" type, personality has the following traits or characteristics: They have a tendency to be impetuous, impatient, and bottom-line. They like getting immediate results; they make quick decisions, question the status quo, manage trouble, cause action, take authority, and solve problems. Do you know why they are so good at solving problems?"

"No," Jim said.

"Because," I continued, "they create most of the problems, and they love telling people what to do.

They thrive in an environment that includes power and authority, prestige and challenge, an opportunity for accomplishment, direct answers, and a wide scope of operations with many new and varied activities. They tend to business first, people second, if at all, depending on how high on the scale the D is.

Because of their 'ready, fire … aim' approach to situations, they need others around them who weigh pros and cons, calculate risks, use caution, research facts, deliberate before deciding, and recognize the needs of others.

In order to be the most effective, they may need difficult assignments because they are motivated by a challenge. If you want a D to do something, tell them it can't be done, then get out of the way! They probably need to understand that they need people, they need identification with a group, an occasional shock, to verbalize reasons for conclusions and to pace themselves and relax more."

"Wow, that's funny," said Annette. "That sounds like me. What is the next one?"

Influencing

"I, or Influencing. Their tendencies include making a favorable impression, talking, creating a motivational environment, entertaining people, contacting people, generating enthusiasm, viewing people and situations optimistically, and participating in a group.

They thrive in environments that provide popularity or social recognition, freedom of expression, freedom from control and detail, coaching and counseling, favorable working conditions, democratic relationships, and group activities outside of the job. They need people around them who can concentrate on the task, demonstrate follow-through, seek facts, speak directly, develop systems, take a logical approach, and prefer dealing with things rather than people.

To be most effective, they need to learn to control time, have more realistic appraisals of others, be more firm with others, implement priorities and deadlines, and use objectivity in decision making."

Steadiness

"The S stands for Steadiness. Without S's, no work gets done. Their tendencies include demonstrating patience; developing specialized skills; performing in a consistent, predictable manner; showing loyalty; calming excited people; being a good listener; creating a stable, harmonious work environment; and projecting a desire to help others.

They thrive in an environment that includes predictable routines, identification with a group, sincere appreciation, maintenance of the status quo, credit for their work, standard operating procedures, and minimal conflict.

They need others who are flexible, react quickly to change, prioritize work, apply pressure on others, stretch toward challenges, are self-promoting, and work well in an unpredictable environment.

To be most effective, they need encouragement of creativity, guidelines, validation, and information on how they contribute to the total effort, and work with associates of similar competence."

Compliant

The last one is the C, or Conscientious or Compliant. Their tendencies include using a systemic approach, checking for accuracy, concentrating on key details, attention to key directives and standards, thinking analytically, weighing pros and cons, being diplomatic, using subtle or indirect approaches to conflict, and analyzing performance critically. By that, I mean most of the time the C is saying, 'I could have done it better.'

They thrive in an environment that includes recognition for specific skills and accomplishments, opportunity to ask 'why' questions, valuing quality and accuracy, clearly defined expectations, reserved businesslike atmosphere, control, and the opportunity to demonstrate their expertise.

They need others who encourage teamwork, delegate important tasks, make quick decisions, state unpopular positions, compromise with opposition, and use policies only as a guideline.

To be most effective, they need exact job descriptions, scheduled performance appraisals, opportunity for careful planning, specific feedback on performance, and to develop a tolerance for conflict."

"So," I told the group, "talk that over and discuss what it all means and how you will use it in your presentations."

After a few minutes, a hand went up. "I think I understand the differences between the types of personalities," said Frank, "but I'm not sure how to go about using it. Can you give some examples of how this works?"

"First of all, let me say that these are just tendencies, not absolutes, and they may overlap from personality to personality, and they may vary in degree from person to person. In other words, not all Ds are exactly identical. There are varying degrees of how much D they have combined with I, S, and C. Each group does have its own unique characteristics, and if you can identify them, you can tailor your presentation to that particular individual. For example, let's say you went up to a D type and said, 'You did a good job.' What does the D say? 'Of course I did a good job! What did you expect?' If you said the same thing to an I, they might say something like, 'Thank you! Now, let me tell you all about how I did it! It was so much fun, and I could never have done it without all my friends!' The S might say something like, 'Thank you,' and that's about all because they are rather reserved and polite as compared to the D and I, but in the back of their minds, they are probably thinking, 'Why don't you reflect that in my paycheck?'

The C, especially if it is a D telling them, might say something like, 'How would you know what a good job is? Besides, I could have done it better.'

The class was laughing as they began to relate to the different personalities and the characteristics of each.

I continued, "What does a D's desk look like? It looks like a bomb hit it. In fact, in some cases, the company would be better off if a bomb did hit it! The strange thing about the D is this: Even though they have a pile of papers two feet thick on their desks, if you ask them for the Johnson file, they will reach in and pull it out! They know *exactly* where it is.

What does an I's desk look like? It depends. If someone important is in the area, it's perfect. But don't open the drawers! What does an S's desk look like? Functional and ready for work. All the equipment and supplies to do the job are laid out, organized, and ready to be used. Without S's, no work gets done. What does a C's desk look like? It's perfect! It's spotless! It's totally organized. With the C, everything has a place and should be in it.

Let's leave the office and go swimming. How does a D learn to swim? Jumps in. Does the D jump in the deep end or shallow end? Deep end. The deeper, the better. First, before they jump, they gather all their friends around. 'Watch this, you guys. I'm going to swim across the widest, deepest part.' Then they jump. Without looking. After much foam, froth, and drama, they finally reach the other side and, coughing and sputtering, they pull themselves out, collapse from near exhaustion and declare: 'See! I told you I could do it!'

How does an I learn to swim? First, they go to the store and buy the perfect bathing suit so they will look good in front of all their friends. Then do they go to the pool? No. They aren't tanned enough to go to the pool. They go to the backyard with one of those reflectors and get a good tan working. Then do they go to the pool? Not yet. They go to the phone. They call all their friends. 'Pool party! Everyone come to the pool party! It will be so much fun! Everyone will be there!'

How does an S learn to swim? Takes lessons. They are great students, always on time. They are prepared, and they have perfect form. They are D's best friend. Because of their loyalty, they are the ones who throw you the life ring when you are drowning from showing off. The I's and Cs are saying, 'Let him drown!'

How does a C learn to swim? First they buy a book on anatomy. Make sure swimming is good for you. Then they show up with a test kit, especially in a public pool. Test the ph, alkalinity, acidity, etc."

Now the class is laughing harder.

"Okay," I say, "let's go back to the office. It's nine AM Monday morning. The D walks into the office and finds that over the weekend the entire office has been rearranged. What does the D say? 'I have been telling them for months to do this.' This is a strong tendency of the D.

If a miracle occurs within twenty miles, the D will always take credit. What does the I say when they walk into the office at nine AM Monday and find it has been rearranged? Nothing. I's are never in the office at nine AM on Monday morning. They are down at the coffee shop with all their friends reliving the pool party! What does the S say? Nothing. They did the rearranging. What does the C say? 'Was this memo'ed? Was the move done according to company policy? Besides, I could have done it better.'

These are just tendencies. If you can begin to understand and empathize with them, then you can learn to present your information in a way that makes it easy for them to understand."

"How do we do that? What specifically is the difference between them in regard to the sales process?" asked Jennifer, who had been sitting quietly until now.

"That's a great question, and that is what you need to know. Ds want the bottom line. At the opposite end are the Cs, who want detail. Therefore, can you see that you need to know which one they are before you begin your presentation? Too much data and detail, and you have lost the D. Not enough data and detail, and you have lost the C. D sellers want to know two things: How long will it take? How much will we make? That's about it.

Show them your past results, give them a guarantee, assure them you will take care of the details for them, and you're done.

With Cs, you better know more about their home, their neighborhood, and the market than they do, which is a lot. Have you heard that they need to like you before they will do business with you? That may be true for the I and S, but not the D and C. They don't necessarily have to like you. If you can bring them the desired result, they will go with you. Usually, with the D and C, it's business first and social second. With the I and S, it's social first and business second. I's want and need to like you and feel good about you. They usually make emotional decisions based on a gut feeling. S's are more interested in your processes and procedures for marketing the property. If you were to rate the four on a scale according to aggressiveness, it would probably be D, I, S, C. As far as assertiveness, D, C, S, I. People people? I, S, D, C."

Other Tendencies by Personality Starting with **D**

Favorite color: blue or black, something dark and assertive. Biggest fear: being taken advantage of. Good with time, usually runs tight schedules, could be late (but don't you be late), will make fast decisions and be ready to act, gets bored quickly, does not do meetings well, skips details, focuses on results, is brief, gets to the point, seems overconfident, may be arrogant, likes difficult tasks and competition, dislikes details and routines, prefers to work alone, impatient and fault-finding, determined and persistent, takes command whether he or she is in charge or not, and seems uncaring in his or her drive for results. In one word: RESULTS.

Other **I** Tendencies

Favorite color: red or something bright. Always fashionable and stylish and looks good. Biggest fear: ostracism or confrontation. Bad with time, usually late, decisions are ambiguous, dislikes unpopular decisions, relationships are most important, talks most at meetings, enthusiastic, usually over-commits, has extensive network, gregarious, develops friendships easily, prefers to participate and interact, enjoys meeting and socializing, optimistic, often makes decisions without considering all the facts. In one word: RELATIONSHIPS.

Other **S** Tendencies

Favorite color: often pastels or earth tones. Biggest fear: surprises or interruption of status quo. S's do things the way they do them because 'you are supposed to do it that way.' Time problems come from over-committing. Feels guilty if late, delays decision making (sometimes until circumstances force it), resists change, sometimes needs a push, concerned about risk, tight with money, nervous with authority, looks to others for solutions, works well with others, patient, willing to help, prefers familiar and predictable patterns, achieves consistent performance, should consider throwing away old files. In one word: STEADY.

Other **C** Tendencies

Favorite color: gray, green, or earth tones. Biggest fear: mistakes or being wrong. Expects meetings to start and end on time, will not be hurried into making decisions, hates to make them on the spot, has acute sense of timing and appropriateness, concern about mistakes can lead to delays, sometimes suffers from 'analysis paralysis,' demands guarantees and references, expects formal procedures, reserved and formal, emphasizes importance of facts, seeks correctness and accuracy, prepares meticulously, needs to control his or her environment. In one word: DETAIL.

"So, basically I need four presentations," said Bill.

"That's correct. One for each. After all, if you are a D, and all you have is a D-style presentation, how much of the market do you miss?"

"Seventy-five percent. Now I see it. I have been talking to them as if they were like me. Now I see that they weren't like me at all. For example, that couple last night. I was on a listing presentation. I just thought they were too concerned about little details. Turns out they *were* concerned about the details. Now I know why. We just didn't seem to be on the same page. I knew we weren't, but I couldn't figure out why.

The same thing happened with the couple three nights ago. Looking at that appointment with what I know now, I can see they were an I and an S. That is why the wife kept asking me about myself and he kept asking about the marketing process. I was told that if I just went on three listing presentations per week, things would start to happen. There may be some truth to that, but it sure helps if you know what to do when you get there."

"Exactly," I said. "The D, I, S, and C are all different. They respond to the same information in different ways. Your presentation to the high-D seller is going to be different than the presentation to the I, S, and C seller. The high-D seller is going to want to know two things: How long to sell, and how much will I net at closing? It will be the shortest of the four presentations, probably no more than an hour or so.

The high I is going to want to know about you. If they like you, you probably have the listing. The high-S seller will want to know about your processes and systems. They don't like surprises and will appreciate the performance guarantee. The high C will want to know everything. In fact, they are already pretty well informed.

You need to know more about the area and their home than they do, or you will lose credibility. The high Cs love their data and information, so this will probably be the longest of the four presentations."

The class was nodding in unison.

"So, what's the one word for you?" I asked them. They looked at each other.

"Flexibility," I told them. "You have to be flexible. That's why I take two visits to do the presentation. First of all, I don't like surprises either, and I don't want to be seeing the house for the first time the night of the presentation. The other thing I am doing is calibrating my audience so I will know which presentation I am giving. I want to meet them first. In ten minutes, I will know if they are D, I, S, or C. Then I use the appropriate presentation."

Betsy spoke up, "What if only one of them is there at your first visit?"

"It doesn't matter. Neither one of them have to be there actually," I said, knowing they probably wouldn't believe me. They had puzzled looks on their faces, so I explained.

"The environment they live in reflects who they are. The house they live in, the car they drive—everything is a reflection. The colors of the house and car, the floor plan, the closets, the paintings, the decorations, the drawers—all these things reflect the owners who live there. It helps, obviously, but I don't have to meet the people to get pretty close as to which personality they are."

The Three Modalities

Humans are designed to take on information through their senses. The five senses are: sight, or visual; hearing, or auditory; feeling, or kinesthetic; taste, or gustatory; and smell, or olfactory. We typically mainly use the first three. We sense things as we experience them, and we often recall them the way we experienced them. Certain smells bring back memories. Certain sounds, like your old favorite song, bring back memories.

Of the main three, we usually have one that is dominant over the others.

Some people are visual, some auditory, and others kinesthetic. When learning, studying, or taking in new information, they will do it through one of these modalities.

Therefore, you not only need four different presentations, you need to be able to deliver them three different ways, depending on whether the seller or buyer is visual, auditory, or kinesthetic.

If he or she is visual, have a visual presentation filled with pie charts, bar graphs, and other visually stimulating material. If you give a verbal presentation to a person with a visual modality, you might as well have stayed home.

People with the auditory modality, on the other hand, will do just fine with the verbal presentation. Practice presenting it in a rhythmic, almost sing-song method.

If your customer is kinesthetic, give him or her something to do with his or her hands. Kinesthetics like to touch and feel things. They learn by doing.

There are three ways to find out which modality people are. You can start by determining which one you are. Go to www.buildmybusiness.com and see the instructions on the VAK Modality button. This is a free download you can use to begin to understand how you take in, store, and retrieve information.

This will allow you to see how others do the same so you can structure your presentation accordingly.

You will also see a list of words and phrases used by people with visual, auditory, and kinesthetic modalities. These are further indicators of which primary modality your customer prefers so that you can deliver the information in a way that is more comfortable and acceptable to him or her.

The third way is to watch their eye movements when you ask them a question. On our Web site, www.BuildMyBusiness.com, you will see a list of questions and the accompanying eye movements. This will tell you which part of the brain they are accessing and whether they are V, A, or K.

It's All About the Relationship

Sales is about relationships, not about conning people or taking advantage of their lack of knowledge to get them to buy something so you will get paid. The reason I like the DISC and the VAK exercises is because it gives me a better understanding of who my customers are and how I can build trust and understanding between them and myself. Shakespeare said it best when he said, "To understand others, first understand thyself." These two tools give me an understanding of myself. They also give me a better understanding of others.

Once I understand, I can approach, present and deliver the information to the customer in a way that he or she finds it easy to understand and comprehend. That is how the relationship gets built. That is how to develop lifelong referring clients. If you can develop thirty lifelong referring clients, you will never have to cold call again, and you will constantly have a steady stream of well-qualified buyers and sellers excited about the prospect of doing business with you.

TESTIMONIALS

"Absolutely one of the best classes I've ever taken! This includes all classes taken at U.T. for my degree! Extremely motivating!"
Chrissy Smith

★ ★ ★ ★ ★ ★ ★ ★ ★ ★ ★ ★ ★ ★ ★ ★ ★ ★ ★ ★

"This was by far the best weekend I've had, and I can't believe it was in school!"
Keelye Acord

★ ★ ★ ★ ★ ★ ★ ★ ★ ★ ★ ★ ★ ★ ★ ★ ★ ★ ★ ★

"Very astute, wise, perceptive."
Thomas A. Whitehead

★ ★ ★ ★ ★ ★ ★ ★ ★ ★ ★ ★ ★ ★ ★ ★ ★ ★ ★ ★

"Came just to get the certificate, left with much, much more."
Bill Damron

★ ★ ★ ★ ★ ★ ★ ★ ★ ★ ★ ★ ★ ★ ★ ★ ★ ★ ★ ★

"WOW! Wayne—thank you for impacting my life and making a difference. I will go ask now."
Jodi Blumberg
C-21 Sunset Realtors
Fredericksburg, TX

Chapter Nine
Negotiations: How to Have It All

"What is the difference between marketing, sales, and negotiations?" James asked.

"Marketing is getting yourself or your product or service known. Sales is—"

"I know what sales is. Closing the deal. That I can do."

"Well, it's more than that to me. Knowing how to ask for the business and how to lead them to make the right decision is important, but that's the last step in the selling process. The first step, and your main job as a salesperson, is first to find out two things: what they want and what they need. Then provide it. Then ask them to make the decision. If you are sure it is the right decision for them, give them the choice and make the exchange.

"Negotiation is bringing two parties with opposite goals together."

"What is the difference between sales and negotiations?" James asked.

"In sales, your goals are the same. The buyer wants to buy. The seller wants to sell. The seller says, 'I want to sell it.' And the buyer says, 'I want to buy it.' They are in agreement about the property changing hands. Now we are down to terms. The seller wants to sell for as much money as possible, get paid in cash, and do it in two weeks. The buyer wants to pay the least amount, have the owner finance it or part of it, and close in two months. Their goals are not the same. Now the negotiations begin. Hopefully, they can find common ground, hear one another, and be accommodating. Maybe they can, maybe they can't."

"How do we bring them together? They sound worlds apart to me," said James.

"The subject of negotiations is huge. We could spend a week just on that one subject. There are lots of parts to it. Knowing when to use each part takes time, practice, and experience. We are short on time, so we'll just cover the basics. These are the six most important basic fundamentals that will save you lots of grief and begin getting you what you want.

"First off, never negotiate when you are in high need. Why? What do you want when you are negotiating?"

"Power," someone said.

"Right, so when your need is high, where is your power, high or low?"

"Low."

"Exactly."

Number one: Remember, when your need is high, your power is low. If you want it more than they do, you're in trouble. *Especially if they know.*

Number two: Never disclose your position. Not before, not during, and never, ever after. Never, ever disclose what you will really take, pay, do, or settle for.

Number three: Never set a deadline you must perform by. In other words, if you don't perform a certain task by a certain date, something bad will happen. Either leave the deadline loose or leave yourself an exit.

Number four: Focus on interests, not positions. Find out what they really want, not what they say they want.

Number Five: Never get emotional. As soon as emotions go up, intelligence goes down. This is the danger in negotiating over positions instead of interests. Once a position is taken, the ego gets involved, and it becomes almost impossible to let go of the position for fear of losing face. Keep asking yourself what your interests are. Are you willing to let a position go in order to achieve your interests?

Number Six: Search for an attractive alternative. Keep looking for ways each of you can get your interests met.

There are hundreds of strategies, tools, and techniques you can utilize, and there are several types of negotiations. Some people just want a good deal, some want to win at your expense, and there are some sleazeballs out there who want to bury you. These six basic techniques should get you started and, hopefully, keep you from becoming shark bait.

One quick story will demonstrate how these can be used. By 1989, the economy in Texas had been taking a beating for several years. Between the oil crash, the Savings & Loan crash, and the stock market crash, it was a difficult decade financially.

Nonetheless, all these problems created a fabulous buying opportunity. I searched for the best bargains I could find. I had wanted to own something near the University of Texas campus for some time when I found something that looked promising. It was a sixteen-unit student housing building in downtown Austin, two blocks from the University of Texas, for $150,000. I watched it fall over the next several months to $130,000, then $115,000, then $100,000. At that price, I could no longer restrain myself and made an offer of $90,000 with the owner to finance the purchase for me at 10 percent interest for thirty years, subject to my inspections. My offer was accepted, and the inspection was scheduled. It turned out the property was in worse condition than I had thought. The biggest concern was the roof. I began negotiating back and forth with the listing broker who was representing the seller.

After several days, he finally lost his temper and shouted at me, "Look, you're getting a good deal. I am sick and tired of going back and forth between the three of you. If you want to talk to them any more about this property, call the owner yourself!"

I asked him for the owner's contact information and was quickly given it. They were expecting my call.

"When can you come over?" they asked, seeming quite anxious to get it over with. We agreed on a time, and I thought to myself, "This is going to be a lay-down slam dunk." I was so pleased I quit thinking.

My wife and I arrived at their home at the designated time. We met the sellers and were introduced to a third person. "This is our son. He is a lawyer in Houston. He is just here to listen."

That didn't bother me as I was negotiating in good faith; however, I did find the strategy interesting. Perhaps this was not going to be as easy as I had thought. After thanking them for their time, I began with, "What is it that you want?"

The wife shook her finger in my face and said in no uncertain terms, "Young man, we are not going to put a roof on that building!"

I was stunned by the force of her answer. However, I calmly replied, "I understand. However, you have owned the property for many years. There is a lot of deferred maintenance, the property needs lots of repairs, rents are low, and, quite honestly, I don't feel it is up to me to put a roof on your building."

I am not sure if she even heard a word I said. She pointed that finger at me again, waved it in my face, and said, "Young man, we are not going to put a roof on that building!"

Neither was I. So there we were, stuck on our positions. I wanted a roof, and they refused to give me a roof. Fortunately, they didn't pull my credit report. I had suffered some severe economic setbacks in the early eighties, and it was not a pretty sight to see. What I also did not know at the time was that they attempted to give the property to their kids, only to have them turn it down. The kids didn't want it! They couldn't give it away, and here I was offering to pay them $90,000 for it! We sat there, neither disclosing our weaknesses, sitting on our positions. I asked them, "Could you please tell me why you are opposed to putting on a roof?"

"We don't want to put any more money into the property. We will sell it, we will finance it, but we don't want to put money into it." So their position was no roof, but their interest was no outlay of cash. Now that I knew what their interest was, I began thinking of an attractive alternative. Finally, after about five minutes of silence, I said, "I tell you what; I'll take the property as is. Forget the roof. We'll close next week, end of March, but I won't start making payments on the note until January. I need a nine-month moratorium."

What was the attractive alternative? Let the property pay for the roof. They didn't need the income from the property; they just wanted it sold so it wouldn't cost them anything. I didn't have the money for the roof, so I needed the income from the property to buy it.

They thought for a minute. "Done," they said and reached out and shook my hand.

"Did you put a roof on it?" James asked.

"No. Luckily, that old roof held for a few more years. I used the rental income from that property to buy this business. The sellers wanted more down payment than I had, but they were desperate and willing to owner-finance it, so all I needed was $10,000 cash, which the property produced in just four months."

TESTIMONIALS

"This was the best class I've taken <u>EVER</u>. Wonderful instructor."
Shani Young

"I would highly recommend this course to every person that desires to be successful in life. The material reaches out to you far beyond investing and covers life."
Stephanie Andrasi

"An absolute eye opener, take this course in your 20s if you can to maximize results. But take it at any age—is a must-take!"
Ron Yaudes

"Great inspirational course. I'd recommend it to anyone!"
Sally Sanders

★★★★★★★★★★★★★★★★★★★★★

"I started my career with Keller Williams Realty in 1986, and I quickly realized that in Austin, to have the multi-million-dollar-producer title on your business card did not mean much. I became quickly involved in continuing my education to a higher level, seeking those in the real estate industry outside of the Austin area.

Trying to start a career in real estate in the late '80s was a career train wreck. The industry did not support an agent to become more successful than their company at that time. I found that leads, listings, and leverage through systems and people with great talent are the key to one's success in our industry. The Austin Institute of Real Estate supports this concept of personal development and has always been an advocate to raising the level of professionalism for realtors. Since 1986, I have continued to raise my production, and since 2000 have closed over 380 properties to date. I have developed a team of highly professional individuals that focus on the three Ls in real estate and systems that support those that have a big 'why' in life. I have brought this with all of my shared knowledge to teach with Wayne and Lynn Morgan at The Austin Institute of Real Estate School to help agents that are either struggling or wanting to learn the key to success. I have led my office at Keller Williams Realty for the past ten years as being one of the leaders in listing success and have taught many individuals in their beginning practice. Wayne and Lynn are front runners that share the same vision of success in their school with wanting to raise the bar in the real estate industry that I share. Their classes are always on the cutting edge in knowledge, systems, training, and practical tools that will enable an individual to succeed to their highest potential."
David Raesz

Chapter Ten

Laziness: The Key to Success

"I don't want employees," said Jerome. "They are too expensive, unreliable, and hard to train. It's easier to just do it on my own."

"Spoken like a true sole proprietor," I responded. "Congratulations. You have officially made the leap from being one employee among many to being an employee all by yourself. That is typical sole proprietorship language. 'Do it on my own' makes no sense. You will never get where you want to be if you maintain that mindset. All the reasons you have for getting into the real estate business have just been negated. They have just gone out the window. What you want to have happen will never happen. Do you know why?"

"Why?"

"Everyone turn to a clean sheet of paper," I told them, "and write down the four reasons you are getting into, or got into, real estate."

When they finished, I asked them to read their lists. This is the list:
Control my time
Be my own boss
Make more money
Own my own business

Most new agents lack the skills necessary to run every aspect of their business well. That is not an indictment of new agents. It applies to everyone. We are all good at some things, fair at some things, and poor at others. We all have strengths and weaknesses, assets and liabilities. Think about it like this: Even if we were perfect at running every aspect of our business, could we feasibly do it? Can *one person* really perform *all the functions* of an organization simultaneously? The key word being *simultaneously*. I have had agents argue this point with me. They insist they can do every job in their business. They have a tendency to act like John Wayne, the hero who does it all. I say to them, "You've been watching too many Westerns." Finally, they agree, with a caveat, "Well, not *simultaneously*."

How else does business occur, if not simultaneously? If you are processing one customer at a time, and you take that customer from his or her initial phone call, through the whole transaction process, and to closing without having, working with, or talking to another customer, or doing anything else, you will go broke very quickly.

Business doesn't work that way. You may have (you *better* have) many customers simultaneously. You will have sellers and buyers in different stages of their transactions. Some will be calling you for the first time, some will be about to go to closing, and some will be everywhere in between. How are you going to keep up with every aspect of this business and have an ongoing marketing/lead-generation system that keeps the engine running when there is only you?

Nobody Does It Better ...

This is the theme song, originally by Carly Simon, of people with the sole proprietor mindset. This is their context, and this is what keeps them in constant physical and financial struggle. "If it is to be, it is up to me," and, "If you want it done the right way, you have to do it yourself." These debilitating, limiting thoughts keep people from achieving their goals because they think no one else can do it or do it as well as they can. I actually saw a printed quote from an agent who closed $25 million in one year. He was quoted as saying he doesn't like the team approach because his customers want to hear from him personally.

This is the classic thinking of the professional, high-paid sole proprietor. He or she may do well financially, but he or she could become extremely wealthy by systemizing what it is he or she does and having someone else do it. I do not work IN my business.

I do not answer the phones, enroll the students, teach the classes, or handle any day-to-day operations. I work ON my business, from the business-OWNER mindset, and put the profits into real estate.

Income Stream of the Sole Proprietor

Below is a diagram of the income flow of a typical sole proprietor and real estate agent. On the up side, he or she is marketing, selling, and producing, getting people into his or her business, getting people to do business with him or her. Once they are in, they become customers The agent stops marketing and selling and becomes a secretary to perform the administrative side of the business, processing the customers through the transaction. The income flow peaks and declines as the transactions close, ending in a trough. Then the agent starts all over again, marketing and selling, income going back up, then declining again as he or she stops bringing in new business to take care of existing business.

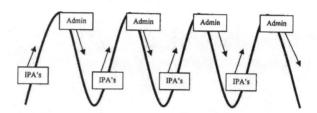

I had one agent actually say to me, "I am as busy as I can possibly be. I can't handle any more business." Furthermore, she said it with pride! That is nothing to be proud of! I suppose in her mind she thought that she had achieved some level of success because the phone was ringing more often than she could answer it. I had the opposite reaction. I almost stopped breathing! I remember thinking, "You are proud of the fact that you are turning customers away who want to do business with you?" If you have a business, and you have more customers than you can handle, what do you do? Of course, you hire someone. If you're thinking, "Yes, but they can't do what I do as well as I do it."

Remember, if you are the smartest one on your team, your team is in trouble.

There are many people who do not have teams. The ones that don't are often in trouble. The reason: They are not leveraged. They do not do more with less. They do less with more.

The Most Misunderstood Word in the English Language

What is leverage? This is probably the most misunderstood word in the English language. It simply means "doing more with less."

Unfortunately, this is a foreign concept to most people. We are taught early in life to work hard and do everything on our own, as if asking for help was a sign of weakness. Hard work is a highly overrated activity. It will not make you rich, it will only make you very tired. The goal is to have enough people, systems, and money working for you that you increasingly accomplish everything you need to accomplish while decreasing the amount you actually do yourself. Do more today than yesterday, with less expenditure of time, energy, and money.

Leverage

When computers first came out, they were huge, expensive beasts with limited memory and processor capability that required lots of power and people to operate them. Computers today cost only a fraction of the first models. The price continues to go down, and the size decreases while speed, functionality, and memory increase. Computers are a perfect example of leverage.

This is the reason I don't work with buyers and recommend you don't, either. How many buyers can you work with at one time? One. How many sellers can you work with at one time? It depends on your systems. You can carry a lot more listings in your inventory than you can carry buyers in your car. Every time you find yourself one on one, you are not using leverage, and you are facing some serious financial problems.

Industrial Age = Work Hard

Hard work is an old, outdated Industrial Age idea whose time has passed. In the Industrial Age, you got a job and worked hard for forty years and then retired. The company and the government would take care of you until the day you died. The way they did it was via a pension plan and social security. In the Industrial Age, these were good plans, and they worked well for most of our parents who followed that path; but that was the Industrial Age. This is the Information Age. Things have changed. There is no such thing as defined-benefit pension plans. They are long gone. Most people know that social security will not be enough to support them, and there is no longer any such thing as a 'safe, secure job.' In the Industrial Age, forty-year-olds hired twenty-year-olds. In the Information Age, you have twenty-year-olds hiring forty-year-olds. The times have changed.

Information Age = Think Hard and Leverage

The new group of billionaires in America achieved their wealth from ideas, not from hard work. Bill Gates, Michael Dell, and Steven Jobs all became rich through their ideas that they then leveraged. They out-thought the competition; they didn't out-work the competition. They built the product, and then sold it over and over again. They don't perform all the functions in their companies.

Hard Work Versus Struggle

No one comes home late at night from a hard day's work and says, "Honey, we're rich! I out-worked all of them!" They come home and say, "This was a long day. I sure am tired." Hard work doesn't make you rich; it only makes you tired. I am not saying that dedication and commitment are not valuable traits. I have pulled some fifty-, sixty-, and even some seventy-hour weeks while pursuing a goal. Sometimes that kind of commitment is necessary to achieve what you want to achieve, but if you do that throughout the life of your business, good luck holding a marriage or family together.

If two, three, or five years from now you are still performing all the functions in your business, and you can't leave it or you have to have a cell phone with you every time you go somewhere, no decisions are made without you, and nothing happens unless you are personally there to oversee it, you have some very big problems. This is the sole proprietor's mindset: In order to make more money, I have to produce more. In order to produce more, I have to work harder. The business owner's mindset is: In order to make more money, the company has to produce more. Therefore, I need to add people to the team.

The Income Stream of a Business Owner
What Are the Facts?

Are you working more or less as time goes by? Are you making more or less as time goes by? When you go home tonight, look in the mirror and you will see the source of all your problems. The biggest problem is that we have been taught that hard work is the only way to achieve any level of success. Hard work alone will not do it. It's an old wives' tale, an urban myth, an old, tired, worn-out Industrial Age idea put in people's heads by business owners who wanted people to think that was the way to get ahead. And those interviews. Every time I read or hear an interview of a successful person, I can see it coming. "Mr. Fabulous, what is the secret to your success?"

"Hard work. Anyone can do it if they just work hard enough."

I disagree. I have found that the key to success is laziness. The lazier you are, the richer you become.

"Nonsense," someone said. I don't know who said it, as it came from the back of the room. I didn't bother to ask because it didn't matter. If it was true for him, it was true for him.

"Think what you want. I'm not here to argue with you. I just want to give you another point of view. Maybe I'm wrong, but what if I'm right? What if you arrive at age eighty, look back, and, after an entire lifetime of hard work and sacrifice, end up with very little, or nothing, to show for it? What if, at eighty, you say, 'Well, hard work is not all it's cracked up to be.' I could be wrong, but what if I'm right? What if there was another way? What if you could use your mind instead of your muscles? What if you could work less and make more? What if you could work less, make more, and have more free time? Are you willing to hear another point of view? I am not asking you to believe me. Just hear me. Hear me now. You can believe me later. Are you willing to do that?"

"Yes," they answered.

"Great! Thank you. I'll start with two points and then two questions."

It's not that I am against hard work. I just hate to see people struggle for years at a job they hate because they were told that that was the formula for acquiring/achieving wealth. That may be a way, but there are others. If you love what you do, it isn't work. If people did what they loved every day, we wouldn't need alarm clocks to wake them up. Especially alarm clocks with snooze buttons.

Point #1

Your job as a businessperson is to get it done, not necessarily to do it. I am responsible for getting things done in my company. I just don't do them. Stay home. Chain yourself to your couch. Do everything from there. Train yourself to think of ways to get things done without doing them yourself. When you develop the lazy mindset instead of the work hard/struggle mindset, you will start to see more and more efficient ways of getting things done. As you begin getting more things done, then you can focus more on income-producing activities and making more money. Ultimately, you will have more choices, and then life really does get easy.

Point #2

You have two valuable resources: time and money. How you spend those are crucial to your long-term success. I want the biggest bang for the buck. I don't do things that don't make me money. The reason I focus on money is because the money I have allows me to buy my time back. If I have money, I don't have to go do something I don't want to do for money.

I work on IPAs (income-producing activities) every day, and I don't do things I don't like. Call me spoiled (what's wrong with that?) or whatever you want. If it doesn't make money or I don't like it, I leverage it out to someone else.

Question #1

Is it possible there could be another way to become rich without hard work?

Question #2

If you stopped working today, would your income stop?

If the answer is yes, then leverage is your next subject. If you don't understand and apply the principle of leverage, *you work too hard.* That is not what you are supposed to be doing, and it won't get you where you want to go. So, how do you leverage your business?

"I agree with what you said, and I'm inspired," said Julie. "I DO believe there is more to my life than just making money, but the thought of having enough money coming in for all my needs, without working, is more than I can get my head around."

"Yes, I know," I said to her. "I find it interesting, though not surprising, that when I ask people what they would do if money were not a problem or an issue, they always respond altruistically. When coming from their own intuition and initiative, they respond favorably toward one another. Ninety-five percent of the people in America can't put their hands on $10,000 cash at age sixty-five. After a lifetime of struggling to 'earn a living' by doing what someone else tells them to do, they still end up with very little. It's an old, Industrial Age idea. Here are some Information Age ideas: Hard work is a highly overrated activity, the key to success is laziness, and you never want to own a business you have to work in. You weren't put here to struggle to earn a living. You make money with your thoughts, not your muscles, and if your business works, you don't have to. Therefore, once you get it built, you are free to fulfill your life's purpose. The only question remaining is, how are you going to leverage your business?

"Let's start with this. First off, what are some examples of leverage? Before we can begin to use leverage, let's make sure we have a clear understanding of what leverage really is.

"The thought of exchanging labor for money is so engrained in our culture, it may take a while for that thought to dissipate. Very simply, what is the two-step process people use to get money? Step one: Work Monday through Friday. Step two: Pick up the check.

The eagle lands. Your ship comes in. Whatever. The goal is to get rid of step one. Make money without working for it. What are some examples of leverage?"

They thought for a while when suddenly a hand shot up. "My sister is in network marketing. She keeps talking about this. She gets a check from her down the line every month. Is that an appropriate example?"

"Did she do the work?"

"No, she just gets the check."

"She gets paid over and over for working once?"

"Yes. The checks just keep coming in."

"Network marketing, or multi-level marketing, or MLM, is where you recruit a person, train him or her, and get paid every time he or she sells something. You get paid over and over for doing something one time. Great example. What's another one?"

"Royalties?" someone asked.

"Remember Jimi Hendrix? How long ago did he die? Thirty-four years? Thirty-five years? His estate throws off about $4,000,000 per year. The guy hasn't sung a song in over thirty years, and he makes four million a year! And he just lays there! That's leverage!"

"How does Madonna leverage?" I asked them. "She has movies, concerts, CDs, books, and videos. Does she sing to people one on one? No, she sings to hundreds of thousands at a time. She makes one CD, and someone else makes and distributes millions of copies. And every time it plays on the radio or someone buys a copy, she gets a check.

MLM, royalties, licensing, patents, trademarks— these are all example of how to use leverage. Design it, build it, make it, sing it, do whatever you want, but do it once and get paid over and over. That's leverage. If you don't use leverage, you work too hard!

The best way to leverage yourself is through building systems to run your business. Then, hire people to run the systems. Clone yourself. Replace yourself with systems. Focus on doing more with less in everything you do."

TESTIMONIALS

"Refreshing/honest/real/funny/brilliant. Highly recommend. What you don't know <u>can</u> hurt you."
Jeannie Resendez

"What an exhilarating course! Thank you. This was very informative and helped me to get out of 'my box.'"
Stacie Dobson

"Very dynamic. He'll take you to the edge. He makes you think."
Dee Dee Passes

"This is <u>not</u> one of those useless, feel-good, 'rah-rah' seminars. It's useful information that <u>will</u> make you money. Great job, Wayne!"
Jay Carter

"This class has given me knowledge and skills, and there is no reason that becoming financially independent is a goal that I cannot definitely achieve."
Sandy Kosarek

Chapter Eleven

Systems: The Grease of Organizations

I teach about systems because I hear many new agents complain about working too hard, not having enough free time, and not making enough money. This process of automating your business is crucial for those agents who have the desire to make the leap from being the sole proprietor to being the business owner. It cannot be done without systems. In chapter four, you will see a basic design of a small business with all the departments. While you are working IN your business, take some time to work ON it. Pick one department to begin in—for example, marketing. You may think only you can make the phone ring. Only you know how to write headlines, copy, position statements, ads, flyers, brochures, postcards, and marketing pieces. If you are the only one who knows how and you don't write a system on how to do it, *you* get to keep doing it!

Legends in Their Own Minds

Most people don't write systems because they think they are so highly qualified, unique, and gifted that they could never be replaced. They believe that the company will surely fail immediately if something ever happened to them and they couldn't make it back to work. However, if you will observe how companies operate, you will notice that most businesses are a combination of repetitive processes. Most of these processes are relatively easy to perform. The hardest part about owning and running a business is replacing yourself because you think no one can perform as well as you.

It's your job to find someone who is capable of operating the systems. Otherwise, you'll find that your company stays personality driven. People will always call and ask for you; you will never have the opportunity to leverage yourself and grow beyond a set income. You can never leave.

Talented People Versus Simple Systems

Hiring talented people is one way to do it. A lot of sole proprietors who decide to grow their businesses are hesitant to do so because of the cost of replacing themselves. Sometimes, you don't need highly talented people. Mainly, you need good systems. Start at the beginning and walk through everything you do, step by step. Write it as a checklist and then test it for accuracy and content.

Give it to someone to follow, and if he or she can do it without asking you any questions, you have successfully documented and developed a functional system. If he or she does have questions, train him or her on how the system is designed and show him or her how it is run. Remember, *the people run the systems, and the systems run the business.* If you really want to test your systems, leave town for a month. All the missing pieces will surface and appear as mistakes, incompetence, upsets, and problems.

In most organizations, whenever there is a problem or an upset, people are blamed. I say leave the people alone. Over 95 percent of the failures in your business are systems failures. Look to the system for the problem and correct it. Leave the people alone. Remember, if you have to think or remember, you do not have a system. Systems are automatic and constant. When do they change? When they cease to work. How do you know they have ceased to work? There is an upset or a problem somewhere in the organization.

I love the story about Ray Kroc, the founder of the McDonald's restaurant chain. Do I eat at McDonald's? No. Why? Because I know I make a better hamburger myself. Then how is it that McDonald's makes more money. Simply put, they have better systems. There Ray was, fifty-two years old, as I understand it, selling milkshake machines. He walks into a hamburger joint in sunny Southern California and sells the McDonald's brothers a machine.

It's lunchtime, so he has a burger. It's a good one. So, he tells the brothers (McDonald) that he likes it and they should franchise their operation. "It will never work," they say. "We already tried it. We almost lost our shirt."

Ray buys the rights to use the name. Then he goes home and goes to work. Only he doesn't start slicing pickles, onions, and tomatoes, or grinding meat. He starts writing systems. Pull the fries in seven minutes. Flip the burger in five. Put the pickles on like this so they don't fall out into the customer's lap. Then he created the University of Hamburgerology. And when people wanted to buy a franchise, they came to the U. of H., and they were taught how to wring every dollar of profit from every square foot of real estate that the franchise was sitting on. They learned to run the systems. The systems ran the business. All the people did was run the systems. And the systems were so easy to operate, any kid could operate them. Then they hired kids to operate them. Ray Kroc built an empire with teenagers! The most unreliable, undependable group of people on the planet!

What business is McDonald's in, who is the competition, and who is the customer? If you said fast food; Wendy's, Burger King, and Whataburger; and people who like convenience, look again. McDonald's is in the real estate business.

The competition is every other business opportunity available to people who want to own their own business, and the customer is the franchisee. Ray Kroc created a turn-key approach to food preparation. He designed it so that someone with no fast-food or restaurant experience could be successful, and the ones who followed the systems were. People with years of experience in the business would call Ray and want a franchise, but did not want to go to the Hamburger University.

"It's a business. A turn-key business. You put the key in and turn it, and the business works," he would tell them, but they didn't get it.

They would look at him curiously and ask, "So?"

Ray would just smile and say, "So you don't have to."

Is your business people-driven or systems-driven? In a systems-driven organization, emphasis is placed on running the systems; whereas in a people-driven organization, the emphasis is placed on running the business.

It is much easier to run a system than it is to run a business. The people come and the people go, but the systems stay the same.

You walk into a McDonald's and what do you do? Look up. That's their system. The kid behind the counter says, "Can I help you?"

You say, "Yeah, give me a number three with a medium Coke." And the kid says, "You wanna upsize that for twenty-five cents?" And you say, "Yeah." And the kid punches a button. Then he takes your money, and the change is counted by the cash register, not the kid, and it rolls from the machine into a little cup. Meanwhile, the kid in the back takes out a pre-made, pre-measured patty and puts it on a grill that has one knob with two settings, on and off, and one temperature (pre-set) because we don't want sixteen–year-old kids trying to figure out at what temperature meat cooks. Then another kid fills a glass to the (pre-marked) line with ice and then fills it to the (pre-marked) line with Coke. All without thinking or remembering. The same process. The same system. Hundreds of thousands of times simultaneously throughout the world.

Awesome, isn't it? Think about it. Four kids: one gets your order and your money, one gets the burger, one gets the fries, and one gets the drink. All in a matter of seconds. Do you really want to do this all by yourself?

A Sample

Below I have included a system I use for obtaining a new listing. Obtaining a listing can be a labor-intensive event. Sometimes the business needs the owner's specific skills or talents. However, in most companies, the same processes are performed over and over again and again. Odds are you do it the same way every time.

If that is the case, write a system on how to do it and leverage it out to someone else to do. This is in a checklist format so that anyone can do it. You will see how I replaced myself in my business. I wrote the systems and hired people to run the systems. Then I left. I even wrote a system on how to hire people. There is a system for everything we do. We even have a system for opening the mail. I hate paperwork, so I had fun writing that one!

A Sample of a System: LISTING PRESENTATION

At the listing presentation:

- ❑ Get listing agreement signed
- ❑ Get Seller's Disclosure signed
- ❑ Get pricing addendum singed (if applicable)
- ❑ Fill out MLS ACTRIS worksheet
- ❑ Get all seller's numbers (ALL—BUSINESS, HOME, FAX, E-MAIL)
- ❑ Get key (hint: make extra copy for the office)
- ❑ Put sign with info tube attached in the yard
- ❑ Put lockbox on home; record number on file folder
- ❑ Take digital picture of home
- ❑ Give seller written list of items needing repair, attention

At the office:

❑ Enter listing into MLS

❑ Print two copies

❑ Put MLS number on worksheet, agreement, and file folder

❑ Make two files: one for you, one for office

❑ Put address on tab

❑   Enclose copy of Agreement, Seller's Disclosure, worksheet, listing printout

❑ Put "Client Contact" sheet in front of file—keep updated
(Document all conversations)

❑ Call the title company and have them prepare:

❑ Property profile book

❑ Order flyers—e-mail with property amenities and picture for flye

❑ Order, mail-out postcards   r

❑ Order virtual video tour

❑ Enter listing into Web site

❑ Put seller into autoresponder

❑ When the flyers arrive from the title company:

❑ Make copies of mailing labels before you mail them

❑ Put labels on the mail-out postcards

❑ Mail cards

❑ Create talking house ad—do your own or download one

❑ Add flyer to fax-on-demand system

❑ Schedule virtual video tour

❑ Put color flyer in each agent's mailbox

❑ Schedule pre-inspection with seller

❑ Check for list of other things to do (repairs, inspections, title work, etc.)

❑ Make five copies of the Seller's Disclosure

❑ Make up buyer packets, which consist of:

❑ Black and white copies of flyer

❑ Flyer titled "Reports for Buyers" (be sure you change the 800 # to you)

Back at property:

❑ Put 20 color flyers in the home

❑ Put 5 Seller's Disclosure statements in the home

❑ Small basket with "Agents: Please leave cards" sign

❑ Put 30 buyer packets in info tube on lawn sign on property

❑ Put up talking house rider

❑ Write or e-mail seller—tell them everything you just did

❑ Ask for feedback

❑ Ask if they know anyone else you can help

Other:

❑ Distribute flyers to list of companies on "Flyer Distribution List"

❑ Send "56 Types of Turbulence" article

❑ Follow up on every showing with seller (if vacant, check every other day)

When property sells: (contract is officially signed by all parties and received by you)

❑ Get receipted copy from the title company

❑ Change status in MLS

❑ Read contract and fill out "Contract to Closing" form

❑ Fill out "Timed Events" form

❑ Put original contract in file with "Contract to Closing" form and "Timed Events" form

❑ Change seller's status in autoresponder

❑ Copies of contract and "Contract to Closing" form to:

> ❑ Title company
>
> ❑ Co-operating agent
>
> ❑ Agent's file
>
> ❑ The office

❑ Order mail-out postcards, copy, mail

❑ Write, e-mail seller, tell them everything you just did—ask if they know anyone else you can help

❑ Follow up with escrow officer, co-operating agent using "Timed Events" form until closed

Day prior to closing:

❑ Obtain settlement statement from escrow officer

❑ Go over contract with settlement statement, double check all numbers, charges, etc.

❑ Prepare testimonial letters for sellers, escrow officer, and co-operating agent

At closing:

❑ Keep process moving, being casually social (it's a business event, not a party)

❑ Obtain signatures on testimonial letters

After closing:

❑ Change status in MLS

❑ Pick up sign, lockbox, flyers, basket from listing

❑ Order mail-out postcards, mail to same mail list as before

❑ Change seller's status in autoresponder

❑ Ask if there is anyone else you can help

Four Steps to Handling Problems and Upsets

As you can see, a well-written system is a pretty detailed list. As times change and the system becomes dated, you'll change it as needed. We know the system needs changing when it stops working, resulting in a problem or an upset. You know and trust that your staff is doing the best they can with the tools and information that they have. It is our job as owners to make their jobs easy to do. If they can't get the job done or a problem pops up, we have a four-step process we use to correct the problem.

1. First, we determine if the person has used the system.
2. We determine if it was used the way it was designed.
3. We look to the system to see if it has become dated and perhaps needs changing.
4. After we determine the source of the problem, we either train the person on how to use the system or we revamp the system.

It takes time to think about all the different steps, but once it is done, I never have to do it again! I can take a brand-new person who knows nothing about real estate, and with minimal training, he or she can run this system, which in turn, runs the business just like I would if I were there. Then, I move on to the next department I want to systemize. Eventually, the whole company is systemized. Let's face it, one person can not run a company alone. With the systemization of each department, I achieve another level of freedom.

To keep the quality high and make sure things get done the way I want, I just write a system on it and teach someone to run the system. The beauty of it all is that problems and upsets are few and far between. The systems-driven machine just runs and runs and runs, quietly and smoothly.

We all have different skill levels and abilities. We excel at some things, we are fair at others, and there are some things we do not do well at all. If you want to build a business, a successful business, focus on what you do best or very well, write a system around the other tasks that you do fairly or poorly, and leverage them out.

We have a system for everything we do and everything that needs to be done in our company.

We Know It Works

How do we know? There are five real estate schools in Austin. We are all teaching almost the same information out of the same books. Yet our company has in excess of 70 percent market share, and it is run by four young adults in their twenties with no business or real estate experience!

"That's great! Maybe I will have to think about that crack I made about hiring employees," Jerome said.

"We even have a system for that. I never get involved, yet the exact person I want hired is hired every time. I don't even meet them until they're on board, but they are exactly the one I would hire if I was doing the hiring. And they are the perfect person for the job. And they are hired in less than an hour with no interviews and no resume's."

Now they were puzzled. "How in the world do you do that?" Jerome asked.

"Simple. I have a system. Would you like to know how it works?"

They did, and I shared my system with them.

How does the hiring process usually work? You run an ad describing the job, collect resumés, and begin interviewing people one at a time until you find one you feel has the background, credentials, and experience you are seeking. You then watch and hope that you made the right decision and that he or she works out.

Well, in our company, we first wrote the job description, detailing exactly what it was the person was going to be doing during the course of the day.

Then, we compared it to the descriptions in the DISC personality profile we covered in chapter eight. What we discovered was that we needed a person with strong primary I tendencies with S as secondary tendencies.

What we needed was a "Counselor," so we wrote an ad that would attract "Counselors." It was a combination of I and S tendencies. It looked like this:

ADMINISTRATIVE

Real estate education company seeks someone who is: optimistic, good listener, articulate, likes contacting people, enthusiastic, performs in a consistent manner, develops specialized skills, helps others, loyal, and can calm excited people.

Call 000-0000.

Practically everyone who read that ad and fell into the "Counselor" pattern called. We invited them all to come in at the same time. We had thirty or forty show up. We put them all in the same room and gave them the twenty-eight-question instrument and gave them ten minutes to complete it. We gathered their answer sheets, thanked them for coming, and let them go.

Then, we scored it, called the "Counselors" back, and invited them in for an interview. We didn't waste time interviewing everyone who called off the ad. We only interviewed the ones we knew would fit into the job description.

Then, we hired our best match. It took very little time, and the "Counselor" stayed a long time.

"Don't you look at their resumés?" Jennifer asked.

"No, we really don't. It may sound funny, but I've found most of them to be a tad embellished. Our experience is that they are not a good indicator for three reasons. Sometimes, they are stretched factually. Number two, their past success guarantees nothing in the future, and last, if they've been struggling, maybe they are ready to shape up. We explain our hiring system to them as a group and give them the Personality Profile, which they complete in about ten minutes, and then they go home. We then score the instrument, picking out the 'counselors.' We call the 'counselors' back for an interview, interview them for about twenty minutes, and make a decision. The entire process takes less than two hours, and the perfect match is made between the person and the job. If you hire people, you usually do it the same way every time.

"If you are doing the same thing the same way over and over, you can systemize it and train someone else to do it, then you don't have to do it anymore, and you still get the result you want."

When you start writing your systems, you may have a tendency to stop because it is so labor intensive. You may even be thinking, "By the time I get this all written down, I could have done it myself ten times." And you will be right.

It takes time and effort to write systems that are simple to understand and implement. However, once they are done, you never have to do them again. And if you do not systemize your jobs and leverage them out, you will be doing them from now on. The system is the freedom. Start with the jobs you dislike the most. Write a system on them and find someone else to do them. You'll be glad you did!

TESTIMONIALS

"I just wanted to thank you for inspiring me last weekend in the investing class. That's probably the best money I've spent in a long time. I can't wait to be free!! It's a <u>great</u> life!"

Ricki Tuffentsamer

"I wish I had taken this course 30 years ago!!"

Gerald Brister

✷✷✷✷✷✷✷✷✷✷✷✷✷✷✷✷✷✷✷✷✷

"A must for anyone over 18—Gives everyone hope and tools for their financial future."

Robin Gulledge

✷✷✷✷✷✷✷✷✷✷✷✷✷✷✷✷✷✷✷✷✷

"Life changing, paradigm breaking—it's a 'must take' class for every real estate professional, as well as every investor."

Jennifer Marr

Chapter Twelve

Keeping Up with Changes and Trends

Times change, and they seem to be changing at an increasingly rapid rate. What may be true today may not be tomorrow. I believe one of the keys to success is keeping myself in front of the most current information available. There is a huge difference between the agent who makes $50,000 or even $100,000 per year and the agent who makes $500,000 per year. Usually, the $500,000 agent knows some things the $100,000 agent doesn't know. Top agents go to seminars, buy books and tapes, study other top producers, and spend lots of time and money continuing their education.

I was visiting with a group of students, and I asked them if they were going to a seminar that following weekend featuring a top-selling broker who went around the country telling people the secrets to his success. Turns out none of them was planning to attend. I was surprised and inquired as to why or why not. "I don't have the time," said one. "Or the money," said another.

"Look," I told them, "that guy has plenty of time and money. That's exactly why you should go. He knows something you don't know. Why don't you go find out what it is? I go to seminars constantly. Every time, I learn something. When it comes to education, you are either keeping up or falling behind. Get out the checkbook and go. Education is one of the highest forms of leverage there is out there. The more you know, the more you can do with less time, money, and energy. Educating yourself is one of the best investments you can make. You may not agree with everything the speaker has to say, but at least go and listen with an open mind. He's doing well financially and is successful in this same business. You might pick up a tip, a concept, a strategy, a technique, or an idea that could make you work easier, faster, more efficiently, or more effectively. You might even learn some new ways to make more money. Don't be so close-minded," I admonished them. "You are all a little young to be so set in your ways."

"No, I'm not. I've been to those things. They all say the same thing," replied one student.

"So you don't think there is anything you can learn from this guy?" I asked him.

Before he could answer, I asked, "Do you know what the biggest obstacle to learning is?"

"No."

"Ego."

Turns out he did attend the seminar. He called to thank me and said he was glad he went and listened with an open mind. He said the speaker covered some listing problems he was having and gave some strategies he could use to get better results.

How Do We Learn?

Over the years, I have observed three things that separate the truly successful professionals from the mediocre and those who struggle. The high-income professionals seem to be on an unending quest to learn all they can from everyone they can. They know that no one person knows all the answers, can solve all the problems, or holds all the secrets. Therefore, they don't see their education as an expense, but as an ongoing investment. The other thing that makes them successful is they are careful about who they take their advice or get their education from. They look for someone who has done it, done it well, and has done it for an extended time. Or, as a friend of mine says, "The stock market is the only place where people riding in limousines take advice from people who ride the subway."

The other trait of successful professionals is that they make lots of mistakes and correct them very quickly. In school, we are taught to memorize the right answers. In life, it is a multiple-choice test, and we don't always do it perfectly the first time through.

As humans, we were designed to learn via trial and error. We are supposed to make mistakes. Unfortunately, most people have been punished for making mistakes and vowed never to make any more.

Not making mistakes is the biggest mistake of all. It means you aren't doing anything at all. There is no way we can teach you how to take a listing in the classroom. It is too sterile of an environment. You must have the courage to go out into the breakfast rooms of America, knowing you may not have all the answers, and do the listing presentation.

When you take this confident approach, you will successfully discover what you do not know and what to correct.

You'll find that once you mess up ten or twelve listing presentations, you will become a top listing agent if you stay with it and correct your mistakes. Very few people have the strength to stand up and admit they made mistakes, let alone apologize for them. Be a part of this elite group that can admit them, take responsibility for them, and correct them.

I am a stumbling, bumbling buffoon most of the time. I don't learn well sitting still in a classroom studying books and holding discussion groups. I learn best by doing. I very seldom do it right, or even very well at all, the first few times through. I just continue to do it over and over and over, correcting my series of mistakes until it finally works.

This diagram reflects a worldwide event that occurred in 1969. You may recall, that year we put a man on the moon. The course is plotted from the earth to the moon.

What percentage of time was the *Apollo* space mission on course?

Only 3 percent of the time was it on course. The other 97 percent of the time they were correcting their mistakes.

Buckminster Fuller is one of my heroes, and I quote him from his article titled "Mistake Mystique" written in 1977. He writes, "Human beings were given a left foot and a right foot to make a mistake first to the left, then to the right, left again and repeat. Between the over-controlled steering impulses, humans inadvertently attain the between-the-two desired direction of advance. This is not only the way humans work—it is the way the universe works. This is why physics has found no straight lines; it has found a physical universe consisting only of waves."

He then goes on to say, "Whatever humans have learned had to be learned as a consequence only of trial and error experience. Humans have learned only through mistakes. The billions of humans in history have had to make quadrillions of mistakes in order to have arrived at the state where we now have 150,000 common words ... The number of words in the dictionary will always multiply as we experience the progressive complex of cosmic episodes of scenario universe, making many new mistakes within the new set of unfamiliar circumstances.

Witnessing the mistakes of others, the preconditioned crowd, reflexing, says, 'Why did that individual make such a stupid mistake? We knew the answer all the time.' So effective has been the non-thinking group deceit of humanity that it now says, 'Nobody should make mistakes,' and punishes people for making mistakes.

In love-generated fear for their children's future life in days beyond their own survival, parents train their children to avoid mistakes lest they be put at a social disadvantage.

The courage to adhere to the truth as we learn it involves, then, the courage to face ourselves with the clear admission of all the mistakes we have made. Mistakes are sins only when not admitted."

It has been my observation that most agents want to know everything they possibly can before they go do something. They have the thought that when they know it, they will go do it. I keep telling them it is the other way around—when you go do it, you will know it. Instead of going out, they hang around the office paralyzed at the thought of making a mistake.

One of our most famous presidents spent most of his life correcting his mistakes. Probably the greatest example of persistence is Abraham Lincoln.

If you want to learn about somebody who didn't quit, look no further. Born into poverty, Lincoln was faced with defeat throughout his life. He lost eight elections, failed twice in business, and suffered a nervous breakdown.

He could have quit many times—but he didn't, and he went on to become one of the greatest presidents in the history of our country.

Lincoln was a champion, and he never gave up.

Abraham Lincoln didn't quit.

Here is a sketch of Lincoln's road to the White House:

⇒ 1816 His family was forced out of their home. He had to work to support them.

⇒ 1818 His mother died.

⇒ 1831 Failed in business.

⇒ 1832 Ran for state legislature—lost.

⇒ 1833 Borrowed some money from a friend to begin a business, and by the end of the year, he was bankrupt. He spent the next seventeen years of his life paying off this debt.

⇒ 1834 Ran for state legislature again—won.

⇒ 1835 Was engaged to be married, sweetheart died, and his heart was broken.

⇒ 1836 Had a total nervous breakdown and was in bed for the next six months.

⇒ 1838 Sought to become speaker of the state legislature— defeated

⇒ 1840 Sought to become elector—defeated.

⇒ 1843 Ran for Congress—lost.

⇒ 1846 Ran for Congress again—this time he won—went to Washington and did a good job.

⇒ 1849 Ran for re-election to Congress—lost.

⇒ 1854 Ran for Senate of the United States—lost.

⇒ 1856 Sought the vice-presidential nomination at his party's national convention—got less than 100 votes.

⇒ 1858 Ran for U.S. Senate again—again he lost.

⇒ 1860 Elected president of the United States.

"It is difficult to make a man miserable while he feels he is worthy of himself and claims kindred to the great God who made him."

—Abraham Lincoln

Mistakes

This article really brought home to me the value of nature's mistake making the process.

In 1943, Wernher von Braun was working on a rocket the German's hoped would destroy London and end the war. Producing this rocket required new metals, new fuels, new guidance systems, new everything. Von Braun's superiors were impatient to move the project to completion. They were angered by the many changes he had sent to the factories responsible for manufacturing the rocket. "You are supposed to be the ultimate brain in this operation—do you know offhand how many last minute changes you've made in your rocket since you started two years ago?" They waved a piece of paper before von Braun. "Make a guess, Professor. How many changes have you sent to the factories?" And there the ridiculous was: 65,121. It was accurate. Von Braun acknowledged his 65,121 mistakes. He then estimated he would make 5,000 more before the rocket was ready. "It takes sixty-five thousand errors before you're qualified to make a rocket," he said. "Russia has made maybe thirty thousand of them by now. America hasn't made any."

In the second half of World War II, Germany alone pounded her enemies with ballistic missiles; no other country had them. And when the war was over, Wernher von Braun became the "ultimate brain" in America's space program. Only a few years—and many mistakes—later, America put a man on the moon.

Adapted from *Space*

By James A. Michener

TESTIMONIALS

"I really enjoyed the simplicity of instruction. Wayne made investing much more clear for me. I feel I now have the knowledge and power to go out and do it! Thank you!"

Debbie Crossett

"Amazing class. I am extremely motivated! Wayne was a 'wealth' of knowledge."

Allison Carlisle

★ ★ ★ ★ ★ ★ ★ ★ ★ ★ ★ ★ ★ ★ ★ ★ ★ ★ ★ ★

"Extremely informative and enthusiastic; he was consistent with his theories and philosophy every step of the way."

Kevin Cordova

★ ★ ★ ★ ★ ★ ★ ★ ★ ★ ★ ★ ★ ★ ★ ★ ★ ★ ★ ★

"Excellent—information far exceeded expectations."

Judd Brook

★ ★ ★ ★ ★ ★ ★ ★ ★ ★ ★ ★ ★ ★ ★ ★ ★ ★ ★ ★

"Very inspiring and high energy!"

April Emore

Part Three

Every Investor's Dream: Being "Inside"

Chapter Thirteen

Insider Trading: Legal or Illegal?

I called an agent recently to thank her for sending us several referrals.

"I can't talk right now," she said, out of breath. I could tell she was on the run. "I'm in the middle of an inspection, this house my people bought is practically falling down, and I have to cancel my lunch with a client because my tenants called, the toilet is stopped up, and I have to meet the plumber at my rent house."

"Good. At least you own rental property." I was in the process of congratulating her when she interrupted me.

"Well, for now I do, but I am sick of it. Every time something breaks, they call me to come fix it, and it seems like something is always breaking. I feel like I'm working for them! I'll never own another property. It's too much trouble."

The Biggest Mistake in Investing

Not investing in real estate is probably the biggest mistake of all. The sad part is that it is the easiest mistake to correct. After all, who is in a better position to invest in real estate than a real estate agent? Agents see the best deals before or just after they hit the market.

Insider Trading Is Legal in REAL ESTATE

I consistently receive calls from other brokers telling me about a property about to come on to the market. They want to know if I want to buy it before they go through all the trouble of putting it through the marketing process, which is a labor-intensive effort. They represent the seller, of course, and therefore don't disclose much about the property. They know that if it is a good deal that makes sense, I am a likely candidate for it. Licensed agents know about property values, so they know if a property is priced high, medium, low, or below market. If they don't know, a simple market analysis that takes just a few minutes will tell them. They know how to write contracts, and they know how to obtain financing. They are on the "inside." It is completely legal, ethical, moral, and very profitable in this business.

Stop Working for Tips

Yet very few take advantage of the opportunity looking them right in the face, choosing instead to make others rich while working for tips.

"Stop working for tips," I told a class recently. They looked at me like I was crazy.

"How many of you go out for dinner?" I asked. They all raised their hands. "How many of you tip for good service?" and again they all raised their hands. "How much? Fifteen percent? Twenty percent?"

"Yes, something like that," they said.

"Great. So you tip your server 20 percent, and you actually work for three per cent or four per cent and split that with your broker? All while paying your expenses and your taxes out of what is left? Stop working for tips!" Then I laughed at them.

I make light of it, but truthfully, that is what happens.

I learned my third year in the business that I wasn't going to achieve my financial goals by just listing and selling properties. One of the downsides of this business is the fact that as soon as you close a transaction, you have to start all over again. Nothing will change unless you change it.

I decided I didn't want to keep starting all over again. I wanted money coming in whether I went to work or not. As a kid growing up, I used to feel guilty about this lazy attitude. Now it has turned into one of my biggest assets. Laziness is definitely one of the keys to success. I have made more money from *thinking hard* than I have from *working hard*.

Cash or Cash Flow?

I have made more from real estate investments than I have from real estate commissions. I take the *cash*, which is the commission, and put it into property, which produces *cash flow*, money that comes in whether I work or not. The commission comes in only one time, but the cash flow from the property comes in over and over again. On that same note, I own an asset—something that feeds me. The beauty of it is that the government and the tenants pay for it for me.

Money Versus Wealth

I remember when I was growing up listening to my parents talk about money. "Those people are wealthy; they have a lot of money," they said. Money and wealth are not the same. They are two totally different subjects. Money is the same as cash—what most people are taught to work for. "Be good, do as you're told, make good grades, get a good job, and work hard for money." This approach does not create wealth but only money.

Wealth is defined as "the ability to survive ___ days into the future." If you stopped working today, did not sell any of your possessions, and did not lower your standard of living, how many days into the future could you survive financially? That is your wealth.

Understanding the differences between "cash" and "cash flow," and "money" and "wealth" has made a huge difference in how I spend my money and contributed greatly to my personal wealth. We take the cash from the business and buy real estate with it, which produces cash flow, which we then spend.

The distinction to be made is the difference between cash and cash flow. Cash is money that is received in exchange for labor. Cash flow is passive income from investments that you receive whether you work or not.

That's why I love real estate so much. Truthfully, I do not know which stock is going to go up tomorrow, but I do know what my real estate is going to do. It is fairly simple and fairly easy. When is your profit made in real estate? It is made when you buy. You buy wholesale and sell retail. Don't pay retail and hope the market continues upward. That isn't investing, that's speculating. Start with something small and simple. Houses are selling for $150,000. Buy one for $120,000, put ten thousand into it, and you're in it for $130,000, $20,000 below market.

From Whom Do You Take Advice?

You have to have the courage to think for yourself and the faith to follow your own intuition. When my wife and I bought a sixteen-unit building in downtown Austin for $90,000, we only put $3,000 down, got non-qualifying owner-financing at 10 percent for thirty years, closed on the property, and didn't make the first payment until nine months later, and our friends told us not to buy it! They said we were crazy! This happened on almost every property we ever bought. We would put a property under contract, get all excited, and take our friends over to see it. Someone was always recommending against the purchase. "Are you crazy?" they would say. That, or "I wouldn't do it. It looks too risky to me." Usually, it was someone who didn't own any investment property—and probably never would.

The income from tenants and the tax breaks from the government make owning real estate attractive. Is it problem-free? No, but what is? There are problems everywhere you go, but just because it can sometimes be a problem is not enough reason to avoid it. Usually, the problem occurs when you only have one house. If you own one house, and you lose one tenant, you have one big problem. However, if you owned thirty houses, and you lost one tenant, that would not be.

In these uncertain times, it is good to know that I don't have to rely on some huge corporation and large accounting firm to tell me the truth about the financial health of the company.

I can analyze a property in about twenty minutes, spend a total of five to six hours on due diligence, and acquire an asset that will perform very well for years to come. Some investors are quite satisfied with 10 to 12 percent returns. Not me. I get a minimum of 40 percent returns on my real estate. Some returns can't even be measured they are so large. With a relatively small amount of money, you can own a rather large investment that pays over and over.

Health and Wealth Are Only Habits

It takes no intelligence to become wealthy, but it does take good habits over time. The sooner you start, the wealthier you can become. This is illustrated in the example below.

Two people decide to invest $1,000 per year earning 10 percent return. Person A starts at age twenty-one and stops at age twenty-eight, then lets it ride compounded until age sixty-five. Person B starts where Person A stops, and at age twenty-nine, puts in $1,000 every year until age sixty-five, compounded, then stops. Who invested the most? How much? Who has the most? How much?

Person A	Person B
Age 21–28	Age 29–65
$1,000/year	$1,000/year
stop	*stop*

Amount invested:	**$8,000**	**$36,000**
Value of account:	**$427,000**	**$372,000**

This is the time value of money compounding. It takes no intelligence. All it takes is the discipline of the good habit of putting $1,000 per year away now for your future. Anyone can find an investment growing at 10 percent per annum. The key is to start early. Once you hit fifty, it's too late to become a tree farmer!

Investments Pay for Consumption

One habit my wife and I have is that our investments pay for our consumption, not our cash from our labor. If we want a car, we don't say, "We can't afford it," and we don't say, "We can't have it." We have a few simple rules in our house. Rule number one is "Everyone gets what they want." The key is that you just can't break the other rules in order to get it. So, if one of us wants a new car, we buy an asset that produces enough cash flow to pay for it. If the car payment is $600 per month, we have to buy an asset that produces $600 per month in cash flow. That way, we get the car, and we get the asset.

The keys to getting rich and creating wealth are:

Start early! Set a goal, make a plan, and stick to it.

It makes no difference how much you make; it's how you spend that matters.

When you spend, is it for consumption or investment?

Are you buying assets that feed you or liabilities that eat you?

If you stopped working, would your income stop?

Your investments pay for your consumption—i.e., your assets pay for your liabilities.

Pay yourself first!

Mutual Funds Versus Real Estate

I consider mutual funds to be risky investments, especially with what has been happening in the markets the last few years. The larger accounting firms were making more in consulting fees than they were in accounting fees and were afraid to lose that profit center and therefore were not as vigilant as they could have been when it came to auditing their customers' books. The fraud that later ensued resulted in bankruptcies, the demise of several companies, lost retirement for many, and prison sentences for a few.

Therefore, I will stick with real estate. There are several more reasons I find real estate attractive. First, let's compare it to mutual funds. To begin with, there is nothing mutual about a mutual fund. Recently, the only person making money on the mutual fund is the person who sold it to you. Here is a comparison of what I see as the advantages and disadvantages of real estate versus mutual funds.

OPM

Can you use other people's money to buy a mutual fund? Call your banker tomorrow and tell him or her that you found a great deal on a mutual fund that you can buy for 30 percent less than its value and see what he or she says.

Will your banker loan you money for real estate? Of course! They are competing with each other for your business.

Control

With a mutual fund, you give them your money, and they control it. With real estate, the bank gives me their money, and I control it.

Leverage

When you buy a $10,000 mutual fund, how much money do you have to put up? $10,000. When you buy a $100,000 investment property, how much money do you have to put up? $10,000. You can own a $100,000 investment for the same $10,000.

Appreciation Velocity

What happens when those investments increase in value? What if they both increased by 10 percent? What would the mutual fund be worth? $1,100. What would the property be worth? $110,000! A 100 percent return.

Cash Flow

Does your mutual fund produce cash flow on a monthly basis? Real estate does.

Tax on Gain

If you sell your mutual funds for a profit, do you pay tax on the gain? Yes. Real estate? Not if you do a 1031 exchange on investment property or live in your home for two years.

Depreciation

If your mutual fund goes up in value, do you get a phantom deduction that says it lost value? No. With real estate? Yes.

Loss Offset

If you lose money on your mutual funds, you can only offset $3,000 per year against other income. In real estate, if you have losses, you can offset those losses against other income. For example, if you lose $30,000 in stocks, you can only deduct $3,000 per year from your income taxes. However, if you lose $30,000 from real estate investments, you *can* deduct $30,000 from your income taxes.

Commissions

When you buy a mutual fund, you pay a commission. Since I am a licensed real estate broker, when I buy a property I get paid a commission.

Add Value

When you buy any type of institutional investment, be it stock, funds, IRAs, Keoghs, or whatever, the hope is that they increase in value. You hope because there is nothing you can actually do yourself to add to the value of that asset. With real estate you can. Most of my profit was made from buying properties that were beat up and then adding value through rehabilitating the property.

I love real estate investing. However, I should warn you that I have not made money on every deal. There were times I owned property that I wished I did not own. Sooner or later, you are going to buy something and feel the same way. Anyone who tells you he or she made money on every real estate deal he or she ever invested in either hasn't done many deals or is being less than truthful. So, even though there have been times when I regretted a decision I made, overall, my wife and I have done pretty well, and we just love the real estate game!

TESTIMONIALS

"Outstanding course. Earned my $ back over and over again. Not just a run-of-the-mill investing class—really an eye-opener. Well worth the time, even for non-Realtors®."

Diane Hastings

"Went into this class with no expectations of what was to take place. By the end of class, I feel that I now have a good basic knowledge and confidence to get myself and family debt free and financially secure for the future."

John Cochran

★ ★ ★ ★ ★ ★ ★ ★ ★ ★ ★ ★ ★ ★ ★ ★ ★ ★ ★ ★

"I enjoyed this course more than anyone I've had in your school or other school. He touched on the 'complete personal skills,' as well as the skill of investing itself!"

Gloria Ashmore

★ ★ ★ ★ ★ ★ ★ ★ ★ ★ ★ ★ ★ ★ ★ ★ ★ ★ ★ ★

"I loved the course! I learned the importance of investing. As the course came to an end, I realized that I made one of the best investments of my life."

Michael Martin

* *

"Psychology of investing is a must-take class for everyone, whether you are a novice investor trying to get out of debt or a successful investor. This class is not a gimmick, but a priceless wealth of information on how to become financially independent and/or improve your current investment strategy. The real-life real estate investment examples help you see where you are succeeding or failing in your own investment. I can't wait for the sequel to the Psychology of Investing!"
Beth Spangenberg

* *

"Thanks, Wayne! I'll make money from this. Hell, I'll be rich!"
Scott Wiley

* *

"The best investment I have ever made! Thank you!"
Lisa Webre

* *

"The best 3-day seminar—a must for you and your spouse!"
Mike Crossett

* *

Part Four

Who Do You Have to Become?

Chapter Fourteen

The Journey to Sovereignty

The ultimate goal is to become a sovereign individual.

What is a sovereign individual?

A sovereign individual is someone who can go anywhere and do anything at any time. They have total choice.

This book and this journey is not so much about what it takes to become financially free.

It is about who **you** have to become.

To become a sovereign individual and have total choice over everything you do, you must first understand that you were born a genius and designed to be an incredible success.

However, over the years, you may have been led to believe otherwise. Abraham Lincoln wrote the Emancipation Proclamation, proclaiming that slaves were emancipated, or "free." However, this did not end slavery. It is more rampant than ever before. The school system is designed to create slaves called employees. That's where the five greatest lies are taught. They are:

1. Be good.
2. Do as you are told.

3. Make good grades.

4. Get a good job.

5. Work hard.

Parents tell the kids to go to school, behave, and listen to the teacher. The teacher tells the students to memorize data. The quietest students with the best memories make the best grades and are labeled "smart." These are the best employees.

Because of this programming, most people have never had an original thought.

Going back to school to get another degree in order to get a better job is akin to fighting for deck chairs on the *Titanic*. Employees have become expendable, and the days of getting a safe, secure job are long gone.

It is the dawn of a whole new era in humanity. Most new eras are marked by a catastrophic event, and the catastrophic event of this era was 9/11. It marked the end of the Industrial Age and the beginning of the Information Age. However, most people are still using Industrial Age answers to solve Information Age problems. The whole game has changed.

Becoming a sovereign individual requires hard thinking, not hard work. It is not easy to become sovereign, nor is it easy being a slave. The question is: Do you want to create someone else's future or your own?

Who do you have to become, and what do you have to do to become a sovereign individual?

How badly do you want it?

The Three Parts to Life

Your life is in three parts:

> Past
>
> Present
>
> Future

Where do you see the past from?

The present.

Where do you see the future from?

The present.

Where do you see everything from?

The present.

Where is your power?

In the present.

Right here, right now.

Your future is created moment by moment in the present by what you do right here, right now. Unfortunately, most people do not know how to be present. They are either stuck in the past, or busy worrying about tomorrow.

This is a diagram of the brain, which has two sides, left and right. The left side is analytical, used for reason and logic. The right is creative, and responds to light, color, music, etc.

The mind is also in two parts: conscious and subconscious. Oftentimes the conscious mind is in pretty good shape. When you ask someone if he or she would like to be rich and happy, what is his or her response?

"Yes!"

Now ask him or her, "Why aren't you?" and listen to that response.

Because of the way we are designed as humans, what sometimes fills the subconscious mind is not times of love, success, joy, elation, ecstasy, winning, elation, confidence, accomplishment, and many other positive feelings and experiences.

What gets trapped and remembered is doubt, guilt, regret, fear, and many other negative feelings and experiences.

If you truly aspire to become a sovereign individual and create the future you desire, you must focus in the present, and to be present, you must clean up the past.

Forgive what you need to forgive; forget what you need to forget. The past is the past. However, unless it is dealt with and resolved in the present and not just stuffed deep down and ignored, it will fester. It will be there.

It will keep you from being present.

I delve into this subject because we have discovered that building our business required being present, and you will need to do the same. It will be like being in a seminar every day. The best businesses are the healthiest ones that come from a management team that is healthy and operating in the present.

Your real estate investments will take care of you in the future.

All of our courses and materials are designed to get you to where you are a totally free sovereign individual in about ten years, or less.

Afterword
Success Becomes Normal

When I got into real estate, I was deeply in debt from previous business losses. I entered the business in 1985, just as the market headed into a steep decline. I made $4,800 my first year. I then began to study top agents and still do to this day. I not only survived, I thrived. I learned how to make money no matter how the economy as a whole performed. When others were getting out, my wife and I were jumping in for the first time. We bought The Austin Institute of Real Estate in 1989 against the advice of others. We used the income from the business to buy real estate. It turned out to be one of our better decisions. We have selectively bought and sold over the years, becoming millionaires through our real estate investments. You can get rich owning real estate or your own business. Owning your own real estate business is the best of both worlds!

In 1987, I found myself at a crossroads. My life was changed dramatically when I was introduced to Robert Kiyosaki in a business seminar. If you are ready to change, pick up speed, get your finances handled, and have all the things you so richly deserve, you can do what I did.

Read *Rich Dad, Poor Dad*, *Rich Dad's Cashflow Quadrant*, and all the other "Rich Dad" books and play the "*Cashflow 101*" game over and over. Then go out and use what you've learned to become wealthy and then make a difference. The world needs you and your gift.

Building a business and being in sales is akin to being in a personal growth seminar every day. All of your weaknesses will soon surface. That's why most people quit; it's easier than handling what needs to be handled. However, discovering what you don't know, or are weak on, can be very good information. Now you know, and that is better than not knowing. That's why you are an evolutionary event—constantly evolving and improving and going to the next level. Once you master building your business, investing the profits, and commit to ongoing educational and personal growth, life improves, joy increases, and success becomes normal.

Thank you for reading our book.

We wish you the very best,

Wayne and Lynn Morgan

Glossary

Admin—administrative tasks.

Autoresponder—an automated contact system used to keep in touch with a database by sending prewritten messages or articles.

Back-end—a marketing technique whereby the profit on the first sale is given away as an incentive to the consumer in order to induce further purchases that will be profitable.

Budget—the amount of money that is available for, required for, or assigned to a particular purpose.

Buyer's agent—an agent whose responsibility it is to represent the buyer in a transaction.

Buyers' market—a market where supply exceeds demand, resulting in a wide range of choice and low prices.

Capitalization rate—the rate of return a property will produce on the owner's investment.

Chart of Accounts—a numbered listing of the titles of all the accounts used in a company's bookkeeping system.

Client—someone who does repeat business with the same establishment.

COC—cash on cash; a way of measuring the rate of return of an investment by dividing the cash put into the property by the cash being produced.

Commission—payment to a broker for services rendered such as in the sale or purchase of real property; usually a percentage of the selling price of the property.

CPA—certified public accountant.

Customer—a buyer, seller, lessee, or lessor who is ready, willing, and able to complete the transaction.

Direct response—an advertisement that offers an incentive, giving the reader, viewer, or listener, depending on the media, an urge to respond, or contact the advertiser.

Escrow officer—person who actually conducts the closing process, obtaining the signatures required from both the buyer(s) and seller(s).

Equity—the difference between the value of an item and the debt owed against it.

Hard money lender—a lender that loans only on the value of the asset, usually real estate, at a low loan-to-value.

Info tube—a device attached to a lawn "For Sale" sign that contains flyers with information about the property.

Leverage—doing more with less.

Lifetime value—the dollar value of a customer to a business over the course of the customer's life.

Line of credit—the maximum amount of credit allowed a borrower.

Listing agent—the agent hired by the seller to list and sell his or her property.

Lockbox—a secure locking device used by real estate agents that holds the keys to a home that can be accessed by other agents to show the property.

Market research—a systematic, objective approach to developing and providing information for use in making decisions about specific marketing problems.

MIP—mortgage insurance protection.

MLM—multi-level marketing.

MLS—multiple listing service; a local database system where real estate listings are entered for sale and made available to other real estate agents.

Mortgage banker—a person or firm that originates, sells, and then services mortgage loans.

Mortgage broker—a person who, for a fee, brings borrowers and lenders together but does not service the loans.

Niche—an untouched, untapped segment or opening in the market.

Pricing addendum—a form used to reduce the price of a property from a fixed price to a lower fixed price at fixed intervals automatically if the home does not sell.

Prime rate—the interest or discount rate charged by a commercial bank to its largest and strongest customers.

Proforma—an analysis of an investment, usually real property.

Prospect—a potential buyer or seller.

PMI—private mortgage insurance.

PSA—primary service area.

Referring client—someone who does repeat business with an establishment and consistently refers others.

Risk reversal—an offer that removes the risk of buying from the consumer and shifts the risk to the advertiser; a guarantee.

Seller's disclosure—form required in some states that is filled out by the seller stating the condition of the home and all the components therein.

Sellers' market—a market where demand exceeds supply, resulting in a narrow range of choice and high prices.

Settlement statement—a form used by title companies giving a complete breakdown of buyer's and seller's closing costs in a real estate transaction.

Soft money lender—a lender that loans money to a borrower, who must qualify for and repay the loan, often secured by real estate.

Suspect—totally unknown person who may someday become a prospect.

System—an organized or established procedure.

Trend—a prevailing tendency or inclination.

TTD—things to do.

UMP—unique marketing point; what a business does or provides that distinguishes and separates it from its competitors.

VA—Veteran's Administration.

Virtual video tour—a video tour of a home that is often placed on the World Wide Web for potential buyers to see.

About The Authors

Wayne and Lynn arc licensed real estate brokers who have an extensive real estate background. Decades of personal experience listing and selling real estate led them to manage one of the largest offices in Austin, Texas. They purchased The Austin Institute of Real Estate in 1989 and built it into the number one training company in Texas with a 70% market share by offering business building, marketing, sales, negotiations and investing courses in addition to the state mandated licensing courses. Now known as The Business School for Real Estate Pros, it attracts people from all over the US who come for the specialized training programs.

NOTES

NOTES